YIN & YANG

An introductory essay on the basic goal of Taoism – to balance
and harmonize the two poles of the *yin* and the *yang*, between
which all manifestation takes place.

YIN & YANG

The Taoist Harmony of Opposites

by

J.C.Cooper

THE AQUARIAN PRESS
Wellingborough, Northamptonshire

First published 1981
Fifth Impression 1985

British Library Cataloguing in Publication Data

Cooper, J. C.
  Yin and Yang
  1. Taoism
  I. Title
  299'.514   BL1920

  ISBN 0-85030-265-X

Printed and bound in Great Britain.

CONTENTS

ACKNOWLEDGEMENT

My thanks are due to Francis Clive-Ross for kind permission to reprint Chapter 5, which appeared in *Studies in Comparative Religion*, Autumn 1975, as 'The Symbolism of the Taoist Garden'.

Polarity, or action and reaction, we meet in every part of nature; in darkness and light; in heat and cold; in the ebb and flow of waters; in male and female; in the inspiration and expiration of plants and animals; in the equation of quantity and quality in the fluids of the animal body ... An inevitable dualism bisects nature, so that each thing is a half, and suggests another thing to make it whole ... Whilst the world is thus dual, so is everyone of its parts. The entire system of things gets represented in every particle ... The same dualism underlies the nature and condition of man. Every excess causes a defect; every defect an excess. Every sweet hath its sour; every evil its good.

R. W. Emerson.

INTRODUCTION

There are two main schools of thought as to the origin of Taoism. One sees it as a development of early animism and magical practices, and to support this theory there is the legend of the Yellow Emperor, living some three thousand years B.C., who was reputed to have been instructed in magic, mysticism and love by his three Immortal Maids or Ladies. Others maintain that although the doctrine of the Tao existed earlier, classical Taoism began with Li Erh, popularly known as Lao Tzu (the Old Philosopher, or the Old Boy) whose date was about 600 B.C. His philosophy was later developed by Chuang Tzu as a rarefied metaphysical teaching and a protest against magic and popular superstitions. If the Yellow Emperor studied magic in connection with the Tao it is reasonable to suppose that the element of magic, so prominent in later, decadent Taoism, was there from the beginning but was regarded as undesirable and irrelevant and therefore expunged from the teachings of Lao Tzu and Chuang Tzu. Whichever viewpoint is chosen, the fact remains that there are no authentic texts, only a few fragments, before Lao Tzu's *Tao Te Ching* and the *Book of Chuang Tzu* and that classical Taoism as it is now known is based on these writings. Never did a world philosophy rest on a smaller basis. The *Tao Te Ching*, more translated than any other book except the Bible, consists of a mere five thousand words, while Chuang Tzu's book, though containing thirty-three chapters in its present form, is thought to have been enlarged from its original seven 'inner chapters' by later additions and redactions; a frequent habit with Chinese classical writers.

In the traditional Taoism of Lao Tzu and Chuang Tzu cosmology, philosophy and religion are closely connected, but conventional standards of ethics, moral humbug and sophistication are mocked while meaningless ritual and magic are repudiated. Taoism is the philosophy of the art of living and relationships; it deals with the whole of Nature and man's place in it. It is the philosophy of the rhythm of life and simplicity of mind and spirit together with the absence of calculated activity, as expressed in the doctrine of *wu-wei*, and the presence of spontaneity, balance and harmony. It is not a world-renouncing philosophy, but a withdrawal from all that is artificial, sophisticated and worthless; it is 'to use the light within to revert to your natural clearness of sight' and 'to live in contact with the world and yet in harmony with the light'. It is a natural unfolding through a clarity of perception and awareness which watches but does not pre-judge or indulge in criticism and analysis, which only cause separation between the perceiver and the thing perceived.

The basic aim of the Taoist is the attaining of balance and harmony between the *yin* and the *yang*, known as The Two Great Powers, the two poles between which all manifestation takes place. This balance and harmony must be achieved both in one's self and in the world until the two are resolved into the One, but it is useless to try to impose this on the world from without; one can only reform one's self and until that self is in equilibrium and has achieved total harmlessness, both to itself and others, it can offer nothing worthwhile to the world in general. That is why both Taoism and Confucianism always taught by example. 'The Sage speaks without words'; if the Sage does not radiate wisdom and the saint goodness, they can save themselves the trouble of teaching them; no one will be taken in for long. Emerson brings the same message to the West when he says: 'That which we are, we shall teach, not voluntarily but involuntarily'.

Both Taoism and Confucianism employ the word 'Tao', the 'Way', which was in use before they were founded and both refer to 'the Sages of old'; but for the Confucianist the Way is ethical, while for Lao Tzu and Chuang Tzu it is metaphysical. 'Never for a moment does the perfect man leave the way of virtue', would be interpreted by the Confucianist as strict conformity to *li* – that is, propriety, morality, ceremonial, principle – while for the Taoist, virtue lies not in morality but in an inward quality of obedience to the Natural, in simplicity and spontaneity. It offers no pursuit of a goal, just the Path or the Way. To pursue it is to put the object as something separate; instead of a goal there is an open-minded experience of, and absorption in, life because the Way and the Way-goer are essentially one.

Taoism frequently teaches through paradox and it is one of its paradoxes that simplicity is required to deal with the complexities of life in human nature and in one's self. To continue the paradox, simplicity is extremely difficult. It is easy to complicate things, to be involved in endless thinking, analysis, pulling to pieces, imagining, reacting to conventional ideas, prejudices and preferences; to indulge in 'something to do' or 'something to think about' instead of stilling the monkey-mind, finding the futility of contrived action which leads only to separation, hardness, ethics, self-righteousness and ultimate strife. Half the so-called problems of life are self-created by this monkey-mind in order to give it its 'something to do' and to distract it from the only valid action, the *wu-wei* or motivelessness which enables it to calm itself and cease its futilities and so see itself and everything else for what it really is and to attain the balance and harmony which transcends both action and non-action and confers the ability to maintain detachment in the midst of activity and the readiness for necessary action in the state of detachment. It also grants the ability to give without depletion or diminution of power.

For Taoism man is not the measure of the universe. All living things share in, and have their place and relationships in, Nature and partake of the *yin* and the *yang*. It is the natural which should regulate all things. 'The Sage follows Nature in establishing order, he does not invent principles himself.' Man's position is as the mediator between the Two Great Powers, Heaven and Earth, and he should maintain the balance between them, physically, mentally and spiritually. He is positioned in the middle point, the Mean, called in both Taoism and Buddhism the Middle Way, between the two extremes – a position which enables man to communicate with both worlds and a viewpoint from which the opposites can be seen as such in their relativity and their contrary aspects, but also in their unity. Man should bring the spiritual down to earth and raise the earth to the spiritual. This is attained by keeping the *yin* and *yang* in balance, avoiding all extremes and establishing harmony. Not for nothing is the Mean called 'the happy mean' or medium.

In Taoism, the primordial One becomes Two in creation and the Two becomes Three and so on in an ever-increasing multiplicity in the realm of phenomena and manifestation. This multiplicity is called the Ten Thousand Things, 'Ten Thousand' representing the uncountable. The Tao, as the One, the All, comprising both the unique and the common-place in the world, exists as much in the daily round and common task as in the finest expression of human genius in the arts, religion and philosophy. It is the changeless source of endless change and transformation in Nature and the manifest world; it is the passive source of activity. As the All, the Pleroma, it is beyond the rational mind; as an object of thought it cannot comprise the thought itself, it can only be expressed symbolically, or experienced to a limited extent in supra-rational states of intuition and mysticism. It is the Unmanifest, that which has been there from all eternity and to 'find' it is only to see what was already there. It cannot be properly expressed, since it is the Inexpressible; Chuang Tzu calls it *Ta T'ung*, the Great Infinite, free from all determination, free from space and time. He says it can only be understood by inference.

The One and the Many can never be separated since neither has any meaning except in relationship with the other. This is seen symbolically in weaving, with the combination of the many threads in the one pattern, the horizontal *yin* united with the vertical *yang* in the interplay of the to and fro movement, the alternating flux, which contains both the possibility and probability of inter-change and ex-change, resulting in the final unification of often apparently conflicting forces. This is well expressed by Browning in the weaving of a carpet:

> ... apart, this fiery hue,
> That watery dimness, either shocks the eye,
> So blinding bright, or else offends again
> By dullness, – yet the two, set each by each,
> Somehow produce a colour born of both.

There is, then, no 'this' separate from 'that', just as no mystical knowledge can be obtained from separateness, from the outside; it must be an entering into, a total absorption, and it is the essence of mysticism that it transcends space and time and all dualities and reveals the realm of the undifferentiated.

*   *   *

The following chapters are intended as an extension of the introductory chapter on the *yin-yang* in *Taoism, the Way of the Mystic* (Aquarian Press, 1972, 1977), showing the relationship of the Two Great Powers to the Taoist teachings of awareness, simplicity, balance and harmony, and their later association with the *I Ching*. Their points of contact with the perennial philosophy in other major religions are also referred to, illustrating how, in many essential ways, they speak with one voice.

1

THE YIN AND THE YANG

Traditional, or classical, Taoism may be the most intellectual of religions or philosophies, but there is nothing one-sided about it: it involves the whole man, mentally, emotionally and spiritually. It includes not only the wisdom of Lao Tzu and the metaphysical poetry of Chuang Tzu, but was also the inspiration for the most exquisite and evocative painting and poetry, which could range from the sublime to the humorous or caustic, and it gave birth to a civilization supreme in all the arts and crafts.

Taoism adopts a cosmological rather than a theological viewpoint as a religion. The creative power is looked for in Nature, not in some outside force standing separate from the thing it creates. 'The Taoist mystic, intoxicated with the vastness of the cosmos and identifying himself with it, felt himself to be infused with all the powers of the universe itself.'[1] These forces are expressed through the Two Great Powers, the *yin* and the *yang*, the alternating forms of the creative force as it is manifest in the world; they are the primeval substance in differentiation, the *yin* the physical, emotional, cerebral, inertia, the square; the *yang* the intelligence, energy, the spiritual, the circle. They are the passive and the active, resistance and generation, kept in proportion to each other by the energy expended. Everything involved in the *yin-yang* concept implies that which is inseparable, unable to maintain itself except in relationship. They are two aspects of one and the same power, but in polarity as distinct from absolute duality.

The opposites have a vital need of each other, just as no human being can live fully without relationships and to attempt to do so is either to stagnate or to court mental and spiritual malaise. This interaction of the opposites has its naive, elementary stage in unconscious reaction, a force impelled by nature but not yet acting consciously as an integrated individual and therefore giving rise to conflict in the two sides of man's nature as well as the conflict between the needs of the individual and society. It is for the individual to find the balance and this requires spontaneous adaptation and adjustment to every situation and relationship in life. It is attained by seeing the extremes, the opposites, and understanding their significance. As everything in the manifest world, the realm of dualism, arises from the relationship between the two polar opposites, the *yin* and the *yang*, it is the main concern of life to understand them and keep them in balance and harmony.

It is a mistake to translate the opposites into 'male' and 'female' – the terms are too heavily loaded in the West; it is better to look on them as the passive and active, receptive and creative forces in Nature: male and female certainly have their place, but are only one aspect among endless others which can subdivide again and again. The active can be represented by the elements of air and fire and the passive by water and earth and so on to the infinite divisions of the Ten Thousand Things, the world of multiplicity.

The earliest concept of these complementary opposites was probably the Great Earth Mother, the Tellus Mater, on whose fertility depended the life of both man and beast. She controlled not only the earth but the waters and as life rose from the waters and was finally returned to earth she controlled the after-life also. Her opposite and consort was the Sky Father who commanded the powers of the sun and thunder, the warmth and rain necessary for fertilization and growth in the Earth Mother. Later, the same symbolism was expressed in Alchemy, in which the *yin*, the alchemical Quicksilver, or feminine power, dissolves the masculine Sulphur, the *yang*, and activates it through tension, rousing it to its true nature; the Sulphur then 'fixes' the volatile Quicksilver and the interplay between the two generative forces liberates them from their limitations. This in turn leads to the presentation of the male-female, heaven and earth as a unity, a single figure, the Androgyne. This concept is met in Hinduism as Shiva and his Shakti; the Sky God Dyaus and Prithivi, and in other religions as the bearded goddess or the effeminate youth, the Dying God who appears in ancient cults of the Magna Mater. It is an expression of the *yin-yang* reabsorbed into the primordial unity from which all emerged and to which all returns.

In one sense the contraries are complementary and co-operative, in another they are mutually destructive or exclusive just as light and darkness cannot exist without eliminating each other, but the existence of each is only possible in juxtaposition to the other. There is a two-way traffic of similarity and dissimilarity, there are complementary qualities but also tensions and a pull in the opposite direction, but it is a tension of balance and not of antagonism and, as seen in the alchemical symbolism, the opposites can transform each other. Creation as we know it can only take place in situations of interactions of opposites, but 'all contraries cease to exist as such at the moment one views them from a higher level than the one where their opposition has its reality'. The basis of transformation and transmutation is the acceptance of the whole with its negative and positive aspects. The *via negitiva* works through rejection of things that are not, *neti, neti,* not this, not that, and the positive plays its complementary part in the acceptance of things as they are, not as it is imagined or hoped they may be. This is the basis of Taoist Alchemy, working on both aspects, accepting and using their com-plementary diversity in the work of transmutation of the individual parts into the whole, the One.

It is accepted that the negative and positive powers can, and do, change places on different levels, such as the emotional plane in which the feminine aspect assumes the positive and the masculine becomes negative; change takes place from level to level, both upwards and downwards. We also see the give-and-take of the coincidence of opposites in the Many and the One; the One gives rise to the Many and the Many finally dissolves into the One; thesis gives rise to antithesis, each implying, requiring and acting on the other until the final synthesis. Everything in dualism is a reflection of the One, the Real. As the moon borrows light from the sun, so manifestation borrows its existence from that which is beyond it and ultimately unifies it. The relative world shines with the light of the Absolute.

It must be borne in mind that the opposites are always connected as well as opposed. As de Goeje says: 'An idea is real only in connection with its opposite'; also, 'one attitude of mind makes us realize the contrast between opposites whereas a different one is necessary to give us insight into their unity'. The enumeration of the opposites would be endless since they run through the whole of manifestation in the physical and mental, the positive and negative, intellectual and emotional, male and female, Sol and Luna, reason and intuition, height and depth, light and shade, outbreathing and inbreathing, the dynamic and static, action and thought, attraction and repulsion, existence and non-existence, and so on to infinity. There should be no antagonism between the opposites as, for example intellect and emotion, body and spirit, work together in harmony in the balanced person. Plato speaks of collaboration between them.

Figure 1. The *yin-yang* in its fluid aspect.

Like water and fire, most things can be either good or bad in their dual aspects and impact; they are neutral in themselves but their effects can be beneficial or disastrous. Opinion, dualistic discrimination, divides people and nations into factions, each having preconceived notions as to what is right or wrong for themselves and everyone else. One must be either 'right' or 'left', capitalist or socialist, fascist or communist, despite the fact that history amply demonstrates that extremes meet and fascism and communism alike impose a totalitarian state based on concentration camps, total repression of individual freedom and ruled by an élite, 'The Party'. These self-same forces can be both good and evil. The drive, power and thought put into any action can, according to the goal of the effort and the intention, wreak good or evil, both for the persons wielding the energies and the people towards whom they are directed. It is the same drive which the criminal puts into crime and the well-disposed person puts into helping others, only the motive and goal are different. Both hate and love use the same possibilities and powers in mankind. In the case of that which is regarded as good, active participation, the positive approach, is considered right. In the case of that which is judged wrong, the negative attitude, abstention, is considered right. Beyond this comes the resolving third, motiveless action, spontaneity, in which a situation is met without either a positive or negative reaction but with total naturalness. But before this state is reached both the individual and society depend on moral codes, based mainly on pro-hibitions which are inevitably inhibiting and are the antithesis of spontaneity. No observation in the realm of duality can see the whole and therefore cannot be absolutely right. It is little wonder that so many of our judgements, both individual and social, produce such unfortunate results when they are based on the erroneous assumption that we see the whole. Many of the problems or conflicts between supposedly contradictory concepts are due to the fact that they are incorrectly posed in the first place and that they are viewed as antagonistic instead of as in co-operation and interplay.

The West has a passion for certainty; it demands a 'positive' approach, a positive stand, a clear cut-and-dry attitude, but life and Nature are full of uncertainties. As Tennyson said: 'Nothing worth proving can be proven, nor yet disproven'.[2] The unfolding experience of life, exploring, advancing or retreating, requires the open mind, a willingness to learn and wonder rather than pursuing a set road to some imagined goal. Hence Buddhism teaches: 'If you want the truth to stand clear before you, never be "for" or "against". The struggle between "for" and "against" is the mind's worst disease.'[3]

Again, the Western mind is inclined to lay undue emphasis on the value of the objective; praise is reserved for an 'objective attitude' while condemnation is implied in calling anything 'merely subjective'. What can, in fact, be completely objective? Even if some segment of knowledge or experience is shared or factual its impact on the individual is subjective. It is impossible to be absolutely objective in most of the things that matter, such as love, devotion, the beautiful; analysis immediately kills natural response. On the other hand excess of subjectivity produces egocentricity and sentimentality. Both aspects need to be held in balance. In attempting to be wholly objective one stands back and looks at the experience or event, stopping the natural flow of awareness and indulging in theorizing or criticism, becoming an onlooker, out of the flow of life: in complete subjectivity, on the other hand, one is drowned in the waters. The resolving third is the losing of the ego in living awareness; of such are the moments and experiences of supreme revelation, beauty, charisma. The supreme identity loses the self and all conscious knowledge of it; nothing remains of either the objective as the thing perceived or the subjective as the perceiver; the subject-object relationship ceases.

Taoism in no way rejects the world of the senses and ordinary life but keeps them in perspective, using them as a means to transcend themselves. Ignoring the sense-world would be to kill the very arts to which Taoism gave birth with such eminent success. The senses are, as is said in *The Doctrine of the Mean*, the instruments of a vital moving power in man which it is his duty to develop. The world of the senses is neither sought nor denied, but accepted. 'Affection and aversion for the objects of sense abide in the senses, but let none come under the dominion of those two; they are his adversaries.'[4] Sense data and empirical methods are certainly necessary for gaining knowledge and perspective in the phenomenal world, but they are by nature naïve and limited and cannot deal with the non-physical knowledge and powers manifested in the mind and spirit; everything earthly must by definition fall short of the ideal; all sense perception is relative and imperfection is inherent in manifestation and multiplicity. True, a vast amount of data can be amassed via the senses and presumably, given long enough, quantitively everything, but this is a matter of quality and quantity is irrelevant. It is the greatest of illusions to imagine that man is no more than his body and senses; in sense perception one sees only results and consequences, not the thing-in-itself. Plato taught that man's elements are in disorder but are capable of being harmonized on the principle of a scale, the senses being the lowest and the World of Ideas the highest.

The senses relay only a limited amount and type of facts, drawn, it is reasonable to suppose, from a larger and unlimited source. The experiences they transmit tend to a pre-establishment and pre-judging of ideas about any person, thing or situation and to fitting everything into an accepted or acceptable framework, producing a mental outlook which is more interested in the shape, colour and position of each piece of a jigsaw rather than the total picture built. It is not possible to get an overall picture through the senses alone any more than it is possible to see and understand the whole of a river by scooping up and analysing a basin of water taken from it. Mencius says man loses his human qualities and becomes an animal when he lives in the sense world alone. This, however, is not altogether fair to the animal, since a noble animal often exhibits finer qualities than an ignoble man; also, his senses are in many ways superior to man's and he has the advantage of having kept the powers of intuition which in man have largely atrophied. Chinese philosophy maintained that the senses should be a small part *(hsiao c'i)* of man. They not only convey knowledge in a limited way but in everyday life are responsible for endless distraction and a dissipation of energy and mind. Hinduism and Buddhism regard them as totally unreliable while the Eleatic School of Greece condemned them outright as a court of appeal but admitted that they have a limited but important part to play; it is only in regarding them as absolute that the fatal mistake is made. 'If you want to follow the doctrine of the One do not rage against the world of senses. Only by accepting the world of senses can you share in True Perception.'[5]

We also use the senses symbolically. We 'see' intellectually; we are 'touched' emotionally; hearing is associated with the sound of the primordial 'Word' of creation and we 'hear' the inner silent voice; we 'taste' the sweetness of love and joy and the bitterness of sorrow; there is the 'fragrance' of happiness and we speak also of the mystic and artistic 'vision', the symbolic seeing of the light of illumination as against the darkness of ignorance.

All these are body-experiences and the body is essentially a limiting and canalizing mechanism ensuring the functioning of the biological necessities of existence in the manifest world with attention to, and concentration on, the thing in hand at the present moment. The body is also an example of the many-in-the-one, multiplicity in unity, no part being able to function without the others, and modern thought now recognizes increasingly the interaction and interdependence of body and mind; health now becomes more and more a matter of wholeness and a break in the wholeness, that is dis-ease, is recognized as being often psychosomatic. There is no such thing as separateness, either physically or mentally; things which appear separate actually combine with other existences, events, causes, in an unavoidable, inevitable and necessary relationship, merging into each other, giving rise to one another to the extent that 'it is impossible to lift a finger without troubling a star'. Nor is it possible to look upon anyone else with a complacent 'There but for the grace of God go I'. It is, in fact, 'There go I'. The universality of the experience of personal identity unites all mankind in a knowledge of selfhood and expresses the all-inclusiveness of life, so that 'when he perceiveth the diversified existence of beings as rooted in One, and proceeding from it, then he reacheth Brahman'.[6]

Figure 2. Japanese stylized *yin-yang*.

Blake, in *The Marriage of Heaven and Hell*, says that 'Man has no Body distinct from his Soul, for that called Body is a portion of Soul discerned by the five Senses, the chief inlets of the Soul in this age'. For Taoism the soul, the feminine *yin*, wisdom, is the means by which the *yang* intellect attains insight and understanding, together partaking of the *yin-yang* dualistic nature. There is also the *shan*, which is the heavenly part of the *hun*, the spiritual nature which ascends to heaven at the dissolution of the body, and the *kwei* which reverts to the earth element. Together they are known as the *kwei-shan*. Of them

Confucius said: 'The intelligent spirit is the *shan* nature, the animal soul is the *kwei* nature. It is the union of the *kwei* and the *shan* that forms the highest exhibition of doctrine ... the spirit issues forth and is displayed on high in a condition of glorious brightness'[7] Ch'ang says: 'The *kwei-shan* are the energetic operations of Heaven and Earth, and the traces of production and transformation'. While Chu Hsi expresses it as: 'If we can speak of one breath, then by *shan* is denoted its advancing and developing, and by *kwei* its returning and reverting. If we speak of two breaths, then by *kwei* is denoted the efficaciousness of the secondary or inferior one, and the *shan* by the superior one. They are really only one thing.'[8]

When they are spoken of as 'demons' the *kwei* merely represent the dark aspect of totality, the irrational, which is why they are feared since the irrational is unpredictable and man generally likes to indulge in the illusion of some sort of security and of knowing where he stands; but in Taoism the *kwei* are accepted and therefore given a normal place and thus robbed of their terrors. In religions where there is an absolute evil, or Devil, this force is immediately turned into a totally hostile power in conflict with both God and man, whereas in Taoism both light and dark have their natural place; or, as Buddhism teaches: 'the cause of life is death', the one automatically arising from the other. 'Stillness is the end of motion, while evil is the change of good; and good is a kind of life, while evil is a kind of death. It is not that these two opposites are generated together, but they are all one with life.'[9]

2

THE CYCLIC

The cyclic view of life is basic to Taoism: 'Returning is the characteristic movement of the Tao'.[1] Life gives way to death, death gives rise to new life; strength over-leaps itself and becomes weakness, success reaches its zenith and comes down in failure. 'Going on means going far. Going far means returning.'[2]

Cycles are the temporal expression of the eternal principle, the Potential. Cyclic time is self-contained while linear time is open and must have a beginning and end. Cyclic time makes the transient subject to the law of recurrence and therefore diminishes the power of death; it takes the emphasis off individualism and places it on the cosmic, while linear time accentuates limits and makes everything once-for-all and highly personal, death becomes a break and a threat. Linear time runs contrary to the laws of nature which are those of the curve and the circle and the 'eternal return'. For the most part linear time is a Western Hebrew-Christian-based concept with its either/or, black/white outlook which has no central meeting point, though Schopenhauer defined time as 'the possibility of opposite states in one and the same thing'.[3] The Greeks largely followed the Indian cyclic tradition of the Days and Nights of Brahma. Hesiod had successive ages; Pythagoras taught the eternal recurrence; Plato and Aristotle suggested that learning had perished and was simply rediscovered.

In linear time the idea of 'progress' suggests that, given enough time, man could eventually find out everything, discern all possible truth. But once higher levels of consciousness are assumed, then Truth lies outside time and not necessarily in the future but in the here and now, only existing above the ordinary level of consciousness. That which is outside time is free from limitations and inner contradictions; hence the one-ness of all mystical experience, a vision which transforms the whole of the understanding and outlook and raises it to that higher level. Chuang Tzu says: 'Man has a real existence, but it has nothing to do with location in space; he has a real duration, but it has nothing to do with beginning or end in time'.[4] But both times have the concept of the Great Year in which time begins again and a new heaven and a new earth come about. In linear time this must, of course, be a complete break, with an absolute end and beginning, while for cyclic time it is merely a turning, a new day in the life of Brahma.

For Zoroastrianism, too, time must be cyclic, since birth and death are neither a beginning nor an end; the being comes from Eternal Time and returns to it. Limited time can be, and is, completed and exhausted, but Eternal Time can be neither completed nor destroyed.

In Indian symbolism time is represented as a deceiving power of the black Kali, the seducing power of Eve, Mara and the Black Virgins, the feminine, *yin*, lunar measurer, responsible for the rhythms of birth, growth, death and rebirth which, in its other aspect, is also the ultimate saving power of wisdom, the beneficent Kali, Mary and the white Tara.

Figure 3. Buddhist Wheel of the Law.

As Professor Needham says: 'The cyclic does not necessarily imply either the repetitive or the serially discontinuous'.[5] It combines the duality of the constant and the changing; the concept of permanence is required to conceive of change, and vice versa. The world of manifestation is in a state of flux against the unchanging background of the eternal Tao, although even the word 'eternal' is wrong since it implies time. In the Heraclitian theory of perpetual flux there is also the concept of the opposite in that flux becomes a law of the universe and is thus an abiding principle. Parmenides maintained the opposite viewpoint, that change is illusory and constancy the real; together these standpoints provide an example of the either/or outlook; both, from the Taoist position, are part right and part wrong.

The circle and sphere are symbolic of cyclic time, as are the turning wheel and Ouroboros with the potentiality of expansion and contraction. The cyclic movement is one of renewal, of infinitude, revolution, change, movement, with endless possibilities, but also with the symbolism of cosmic completion. The straight line of the square or cube represents the finite, the limited, the temporal; it belongs to the earth, the static, and symbolizes law and order. The circle or sphere are perfection, 'rounded off'. Roundness has always had a sacred quality and is the most natural shape in nature.

Cycles of time contain all alternations, the seasons, darkness and light, the dawn and dusk which precede the days and nights of cyclic manifestation. Twilight is the period of increasing density, of deepening obtuseness, insensitivity and non-awareness, such as the present age of the Kali Yuga, before the dawn and reawakening of the new age in the law of universal reversion.

The cyclic is the very form and nature of the Ta Ki, with its alternation of dark and light, contraction and expansion, inaction and action. 'The ends and origins of things have no limit from which they began. The origin of one thing may be the considered end of another; the end of one may be considered the origin of the next. Who can distinguish accurately between the cycles?'[6] 'Each in turn gives birth to the next and is overcome by the next in turn.'[7] This is the teaching of the Five Elements School in Taoism. The Five Elements constitute the forces of Nature, controlling both the natural and the human world, they are divisions arising from the primordial substance as it develops and becomes differentiated and diffused in the manifest world. They are the Agents or Movers and are the basic composition of the universe, the ultimate simplicity, that which is not reducible to anything else. Each in turn controls a cycle of history, forming a total cyclic succession and each giving way in turn to the other. Four of the elements occupy the cardinal points and represent the seasons, the fifth element, the earth, is at the centre.

North
WATER
Mercury
Winter. Cold. Black.

West		EARTH	East
METAL		EARTH	WOOD
Venus		Centre	Jupiter
Autumn. Destruction. White.		Saturn	Spring. Production. Green.
		Yellow	

South
FIRE
Mars
Summer. Heat. Red.

The cyclic viewpoint naturally implies the metaphysical doctrine of the Centre, found in all Eastern religions with the exception of Zoroastrianism. This Centre is the Eye of the Heart, the centre of balance; it is a concept beyond the rational mind since the lesser cannot comprehend the greater. As the pivotal point of balance it is the possibility of expansion, also the point of control of the circle as well as of the spiral; it is the point from which all force eminates and to which all returns. Again, it is the place where the opposing forces come to rest in perfect equilibrium; to attain this 'point quiescent' they must have achieved equal strength and be in absolute balance. Here the pull and tensions of opposites are finally resolved. The Centre is the focal point of energy, the place of resolution of the passive and active, the *yin* and the *yang*, the point of stillness and hence of receptivity, the point from which it is possible to see things whole, while from the circumference different and distorted views are obtained. At this point desire ceases and being takes over; it is the place of peace which passes understanding.

In Taoism, man is held to occupy the central position since he is mediator between Heaven and Earth and on his maintenance of the balance between the *yin* and the *yang* depends not only his own spiritual, mental and physical health, but that of the world about him; he is capable of making or marring both from his central position. If he swings between the two poles he finds himself removed from the Centre and, obviously, the further from the Centre the greater the imbalance. From imbalance comes failure and hence discontent. Nothing can endure for long when out of balance and harmony since it will break down first in friction and frustration and then in violence. Once duality loses its balance it falls into extremes and the opposites then become antagonistic and destructive instead of co-operative and creative. All happiness, all wisdom, depends on the balance and harmony of the opposites, first in their recognition and then in their reconciliation. Man naturally and rightly feels himself the centre and in his religious life strives towards the spiritual Centre which is at one and the same time the centre of man, of the world and of all things. Eliade warns against envisaging this Centre as a geometrical position; it is an experience, he points out that all oriental civilizations recognize an unlimited number of centres, all even called the Centre of the World, but all being sacred space consecrated by a hierophany. The spiritual quest is the journey back to the Centre and all myths and symbols stress the difficulty of attaining it, which is why all pilgrimage was made symbolically arduous. The return to the Centre is the journey home, back to the central hearth. Ulysses, Parsifal, all those in quest of the Grail, the source of immortality and life, were in search of the Cosmic Centre. Or, as T.S. Eliot put it, it is necessary to go a long way, through many difficulties, to find a place one has never left.

The labyrinth is a symbol of the trials endured in attaining the Centre and it was sometimes walked as such in mediaeval Christian cathedrals, as at Chartres, by people who for various reasons were unable to undertake an actual journey to some sacred Centre, such as a shrine or holy well or place of miracles. The way to the centre of the labyrinth is also the way back to Paradise, the Cosmic Centre, where man and the divine meet. The circle of the labyrinth is time and its continuous line is eternity and the Centre, as has been said, is the principle of equilibrium, non-manifestation, the re-conciliation of opposites, the Quintessence of the Alchemists and Aristotle's 'Unmoved Mover'. Taoism calls the perfect Sage 'he who has entered the state of repose'; it is 'to return to one's roots', passing from the moving circumference of the cosmic wheel to the unmoving Centre which unites all. This is also the primordial state which Hinduism calls *balya*, childhood, and of which Christianity says that 'except ye become as little children' it is impossible to reach the Kingdom of Heaven, the Centre. In Hinduism this Point represents Unity, Pure Being, Ishwara, while in Qabalism before the Point, the One, there is only the Ain, the incomparable Absolute, the ultimate mystery. The hidden point is also Thought. 'Everything without exception was first conceived in Thought. And if anyone should say "Lo, there is something new in the world", impose silence on him, for the thing was previously conceived in Thought.' This philosophical viewpoint is also familiar in Plato's theory of Ideas. In Islam the Point at the Centre is the Divine Abode, the Divine Station, where there are no longer any contraries. The further any being is 'off-centre' the greater the disorder and unbalance, mentally and spiritually. In Taoism Chuang Tzu says: 'This point is the Pivot of the Law; it is the motionless centre of a circumference on the rim of which all contingencies, distinctions and individualities resolve; and from it only Infinity is to be seen, which is neither this nor that, nor yes nor no. To see all in the yet indifferentiated primordial unity, or from such a distance that all melts into one, this is true intelligence.'

3

BALANCE AND HARMONY

Life should be, as Chuang Tzu puts it, 'The blended harmony of the *yin* and the *yang*'. In the time of the Sages of Old there was said to be perfect harmony which was expressed in the *Li Chi*, or Book of Rites as follows:

> When the Great Tao prevailed the whole world was one community. Men of talent and virtue were chosen to lead the people, their words were sincere and they cultivated harmony. Men treated the parents of others as their own and cherished the children of others as their own. Proper provision was made for the aged until their death, work was provided for the able-bodied and education for the young; kindness and compassion were shown to widows, orphans, childless men and those disabled by disease, so that all were looked after. For every male there was a division of land; for every female a home. The people disliked to have wealth wasted but they did not hoard it up for themselves; they disliked to have their talents unemployed, but they did not work solely for themselves; hence all cunning designs became useless and theft and banditry did not exist. The outer doors of houses remained open and were never shut ...this was called 'the Age of Great Universality'.

This was no communist concept since this universal good and the 'one community' provided not only material well-being but maintained individual freedom and independence for each to develop his own potential. Balance and harmony have to be found first in the smallest unit, the individual, otherwise unbalanced individuals can, and do, largely dominate the governments of the world. Totalitarian societies, whether fascist or communist, are all inaugurated and ruled by power maniacs prepared to maintain their rule by wholesale cunning, deceit and murder, and, as it has been said, the history of mankind is largely the history of the rule of the pathological over the normal. To desire power over others is already a pathological state of mind and totally different from the Sage who wishes to see man first understand and rule himself and then bring about the reign of universal benevolence, a condition which is best defined by the Chinese *jen* which, though difficult to translate, implies so much more than 'man', signifying also universal man, an all-embracing humanity which includes the individual and his relationship with society and society paying its debt to the individual; ideal humanity, showing a sense of compassion for and sympathy with all life. But this can only be done through small groups. Giant organizations, although often claiming to be universal and democratic, cannot maintain the individual touch and can be dominated and manipulated by cliques or a dictatorship. Dr E.F. Schumacher has already sounded this warning in the West and Sri Guru Dutt in the Saraswat Community in India, that vast modern societies present a solid mass which is never broken up into smaller groups to which people can 'belong', or to which they can return 'to introduce sanity and order and discipline into its over-exerted mind'. In the midst of this dehumanization and disintegration all giant organisms use dubious, if not positively unscrupulous, methods of manipulation of the masses. Harmony requires that each part should fulfil its particular function in relationship to the whole and that the whole should be committed to the good of the part. At one extreme society imposes absolute conditions and the individual ceases to matter, as in the totalitarian ant-heap states; on the other side stand the drop-out and the criminal, totally rejecting society's legitimate claims in favour of unlicenced individualism. But the modern drop-out is in no sense analogous with the Taoist hermit who chose to leave urban society. The hermit made no demands upon other people to keep him; he kept himself and did not reject society when it came to him in the form of other philosophers, poets or disciples.

In Greek thought, particularly in the Platonic and Pythagorean schools, the 'good' is represented not merely as morality but as proportion and harmony; it also implies law and order. Harmony is not an emotional or pleasure-giving response, though emotional balance would be impossible without it, but a mind-controlled and universal necessity, exacting in its demands and severe in its repercussions with natural punitive consequences if the laws of balance and harmony are disobeyed. Taoism is sometimes accused of anarchy, but anarchy is by definition disorder and confusion while Taoism demands obedience to the laws of Nature and the laws of man may only be ignored if they run contrary to Nature and therefore to harmony. Since there is no harmony possible without relationship harmony in Nature must involve the Ten Thousand Things, and man, fallen into the realm of multiplicity, is responsible for the maintenance of harmony in living according to Nature and the *yin-yang* interplay and balance.

Confucius associated morality with harmony and the balanced outlook of the Perfect Man. 'The ability to recognize the parallel to one's own case may be called the secret of goodness.' When a disciple asked about virtue Confucius replied: 'It is, when you go abroad, to behave to everyone as if you were receiving a great guest ... and ... not to do to others as you would not wish done to yourself'.[1] 'Now the man of perfect virtue, wishing to be established himself, seeks also to establish others; wishing to be enlarged himself, he seeks to enlarge others. To be able to judge of others by what is nigh in ourselves, this may be called the art of virtue'.[2]

Tzu Ssu, a grandson of Confucius, to whom *The Doctrine of the Mean* was attributed, said: 'Harmony is the universal path which all should pursue'. While Mencius wrote that 'The Superior Man cultivates a friendly harmony without being weak ... he stands erect without inclining to either side'. 'In a high situation he does not treat with contempt his inferiors. In a low situation he does not court the favour of his superiors.'

Confucianism, though not strictly speaking a religion, later became the semblance of one, having temples devoted to Confucian and ancestral 'reverence' rather than the more devotional 'worship'; but even in the temples Confucianism retained its austere character and there were no images, only a solitary Tablet of Confucius. Yet, although Confucius avoided any discussion of the supernatural or the spiritual, his system might be considered religious in that it stood for fixed beliefs concerning the Absolute and man's place in the universe as mediator between Heaven and Earth. The Supreme Power, *Tien*, is impersonal, though endowed with consciousness.

Confucianism represents the practical, sober, social side of Chinese life and character, balanced by Taoism in the metaphysical, artistic and light-hearted aspect. It is a system of social, moral and political order based on the impeccable conduct of the scholar-gentleman also called the Superior Man or Perfect Man; an aristocracy of intellect attainable by anyone with the necessary abilities and character. The system involved ritual, deportment and propriety and used music and poetry for those ends. Every movement was a ritual and everything symbolic. For example, the robe worn by the scholar-gentleman was in itself a moral symbol. The roundness of the sleeves represented the manners in the elegance and perfection of the circle. The straightness of the seams depicted justice and incorruptibility and the edge of the robe, horizontal like the beam of a balance, was firmness. All colours and designs also held their symbolism.

Of himself, Confucius said: 'I transmit, I do not create', and his work was primarily historical and socio-political, based on Li, which like Tao, is almost impossible to translate, having too wide a meaning. Socially it is faultless conduct and good manners, a courtesy which puts others before oneself. Historically and politically it implies an ideal order and rigid self discipline. 'One should so live that one is at ease and in harmony with the world, without loss of happiness.' Like Taoism, Confucianism teaches by example and the philosopher must live his convictions. 'The man of moral virtue, wishing to stand firm himself, will lend firmness to others. Wishing himself to be illuminated, he will illuminate others. To be able to do to others as we would be done by, this is the true token of moral virtue.'

Figure 4. The Tablet of Confucius. Interior of the Confucian Temple at Pekin (from a rare photograph).

A profound student of the *I Ching*, Confucius wrote ten commentaries on it. The *T'ai Ch'i*, Primordial Unity, descending into duality, the *yin* and the *yang*, produced the Four Designs which gave rise to the Eight Diagrams, the *Pa Kua*, representing primordial unity and manifest diversity in all possible pairs of opposites and their permutations and combinations.

This may also be arranged as:

K'un	Kên	K'an	Sun	Chên Li		Tui	Ch'ien
☷	☶	☵	☴	☳ ☲		☱	☰
Greater Yin		Lesser Yang		Lesser Yin		Greater Yang	
YIN				YANG			

Figure 5. Pa Kua and yin-yang.

The Taoist Sage, who is the 'Perfect' or 'Superior' Man of Confucianism, is the one who has gone through 'civilization' and come out on the other side; his whole life is held in balance and harmony, he neither wants 'status', that social disease which is the product of a total imbalance in values, nor does he want more than enough of anything. He does not strain after money in excess of his needs or persuade himself that luxuries are necessities to the point where excess takes over and simplicity is lost and quantity, not quality, becomes the norm. By demanding and taking too much, one actually gets less, in human relationships, in Nature, or the land; any over-demanding results in retraction, imbalance and loss. Reciprocity is essential; as much must be put back as is taken out.

On the other hand the Sage is no ascetic, merely someone

who chooses to live simply, which can be achieved in any environment, either rural or urban. Asceticism is at the least unnecessary; it is the forcing of natural tendencies into a strait-jacket and confuses self-control with self-subjugation in terms of victor and vanquished, a state which sets up opposition instead of co-operation; it is a violent renunciation instead of a gentle and timely letting-go. Mortification of the flesh is also likely to produce bodily malaise and mental self-righteousness. The body should not be subjected to unnaturally restrictive practices but kept in good order as a balanced support for mind and spirit, this was the aim of Taoist yoga.

The Tao is everywhere and unlimited, there is no need to seek it along narrow and limited paths. As Martin Buber said: 'In asceticism the spiritual being shrinks, sleeps, becomes empty and bewildered; only in joy can it awaken and fulfil itself until free from all lack, it matures to the divine'.[3] There is no need for asceticism and renunciation since undesirable qualities will die naturally when the sense of values is changed. When the being is orientated to the true nature of things the false will simply fall away. But there is a need for joy, the sages and poets of both East and West are at one on that point. 'How can one calculate all the joys? Therefore the Sage roams with light heart through the universe, in which nothing can be lost because all is preserved. He finds early death good, old age, his beginning and his end good.' This is what Maspero describes as 'the quality of mystical joy which characterizes Taoist thought', and Creel, on the same subject, says the Taoist has 'an apparent simplicity that is wholly deceptive ... and ... an approach to the ridiculous that always characterizes the sublime'.[4] A person without a sense of humour suffers from a deficiency and all deficiency is, by definition, a lack of wholeness and balance. Joy is a vital quality, an important experience, balancing the sorrow in life, but it has the added advantage of being cumulative. The Chinese have a saying that a sorrow shared is a sorrow halved; a joy shared is a joy doubled; and again, 'The Ancients caused the people to have pleasure as well as themselves and therefore they could enjoy it'.

An inward joyousness arises from an inner assurance and is an essential ingredient for serenity, for the easing of tensions, for the letting-go of *wu-wei* and the abandoning of useless anxieties and worries. Hesketh Pearson, writing on Oscar Wilde, says: 'The great humorist raises commonsense to poetry, lifts the burden of life, releases the spirit, imparts happiness, creates brotherhood and cleanses the mind of cant, pretentiousness and conceit. He is the chief civilizing force in humanity, the real democrat and equalitarian, detested and dreaded by tyrants and humbugs ... we know what serious people have made of the world, but we shall never know what the humorous people would make of it, because the world will never be intelligent enough to give them a chance, and they would be too intelligent to take it.'[5] In India Tagore wrote: 'From joy does spring all this creation, by joy it is maintained, towards joy does it progress and into joy does it enter.'[6] Which echoes the *Chandogya Upanishad*: 'Brahman is life, Brahman is the Void ... Joy, verily, that is the same as the Void, the Void, verily, that is the same as joy'.

(a)   (b)

Figure 6. (a) *Yin-yang.* Immutable. Absolute.
(b) *Yin-yang.* Movable. Relative.

In the I-Thou situation in the manifest world, sharing and giving are both expressions of joy in unity. The dualistic situation of possessiveness has been surmounted, superceded and transmuted into an open, satisfying possession in which each is equally possessed in oneness, whereas material possessiveness operates a law of diminishing returns: much wants more, appetite is never satisfied, envy enters, the ego hardens and joy vanishes.

There is also joy in the prodigal beauty of the natural world which has nothing to do with materialistic usefulness. As Ruskin says: 'They have no connection ... you were made for enjoyment, the most beautiful things in the world are the most useless – peacocks and lilies, for instance'.[7] He also remarks that 'We need examples of people who, leaving heaven to decide whether they are to rise in the world, decide for themselves that they will be happy in it and have resolved to seek, not greater wealth but simpler pleasure, not higher fortune but deeper felicity, making the first of possessions self-possession'. There is no sillier pursuit than that of happiness, which must be spontaneous and rise from within, from that Kingdom of Heaven. Like its opposite, sorrow, it has no life of its own but must be the outcome of awareness and acceptance, 'a lyrical, almost ecstatic acceptance', which Arthur Waley found particularly exemplified in Chuang Tzu.

Happiness, for both individual and society, depends largely on love, but it is not always realized that to love others *as* one's self it is necessary to start with one's self. One cannot love others without first experiencing the rudimentary love of self and having an integrated self to respect and love before both can be lost in the wider universal love. St Augustine maintained that the right kind of love starts with one's self *(ordinata dilectio)* before it can be extended to others. From here he, like the Taoists, indicates that it should go beyond those loved naturally to the extent of loving one's enemies. Aristotle says that only the wise man is capable of loving himself. 'The bad man ... being ever at strife with himself, can never be his own friend.'[8] The misanthrope, and the radically pessimistic person, turns against himself and 'annihilates all he does'; he is interested at the same time in his own destruction and his own preservation ... this volition is a never-ending contradiction in itself'.[9] He has started by hating and damaging himself and therefore continues by damaging others; but to damage one is to damage all since one's neighbour *is* one's self. This is no do-gooding concern for others but the realization of the unity of all life, human, animal and vegetable, and the recognition of total involvement in it. 'He who sees everyone in himself and himself in everyone, thus seeing the same God living in all, he, the Sage, no more kills the self by the self.'[10]

4

HARMLESSNESS
AND NON-VIOLENCE

Harmlessness, non-violence, *ahimsa*, is, in Taoist, Vedic, Jain and Buddhist tradition, 'not to cause suffering to living beings by speech, mind or body'.[1] As with love, so with harmlessness: 'all beings' include one's self and all forms of life. To harm one's self is to harm part of society; violence against society is violence to one's self; the two are inseparable. The basis of all true morality is founded on relationships, the sense of oneness; it is this which transcends the ego-centred personality and gives a sense of belonging, which thus imposes its sanctions of harmlessness. The Jains maintain that the violent man injures himself, even if he does not succeed in injuring others, whilst the Puranas assert that those who employ and delight in violence do not live long – obviously, since they set in motion a train of destructive forces in which they are involved and which must rebound on them. There is also in violence a too-rapid expenditure of forces and energy which become exhausted and burn out. But harmlessness is not sufficient in itself unless it produces good-will, consideration and compassion. The negative quality of non-violence must be balanced by the positive aspect of compassion and all that is conducive to the well-being and happiness of both the individual and society. The Buddhaghosa says: 'Compassion is based on seeing the helplessness of those overcome by suffering and it results in abstention from harming others'. And in listing the 'pairs of opposites', the *Altar Sutra* places compassion as the contrary of harmfulness.

Violence sets up a vicious circle, leading to counter-measures, retaliation, revolution and counter-revolution. True non-violence depends on discipline and self-control. Eastern religions teach that violence must be eradicated; its roots must be cut by control of thought, which is the first stage before any action. In violence, the extremes meet in the hectoring bully and the coward. Mahatma Ghandi, writing on non-violence, said that the coward, seeking protection, cannot be non-violent but encourages aggression; of violence and cowardice, he found the latter the worse evil.

Harmful qualities, leading to violence, are fear, envy, greed of possession, the worship of status and luxury, the over-balance of any excess. Capitalism, Socialism, Communism, all, despite disclaimers, subscribe to the same violence-producing aims of ever-increasing productivity, 'progress' and material prosperity, which does not stop at enough but makes endless demands for higher and higher material standards and ignores the vital part of man in the mental and spiritual development. Once the basic needs of all living beings – food, warmth and shelter – are met, which any reasonable society admits they should be, the emphasis should be taken off the material and turned to even more fundamental needs, self-fulfilment and realization through the arts and crafts and things of the mind and spirit, all things which require individual discipline but give basic satisfaction, integrating the person and fulfilling the potential, without which any human being is incomplete. Only a small integrated community, in touch with the land, can produce anything like these ideal results. Industrialism, be it capitalist or communist controlled, produces the inequalities of a population of slaves to the machine and the inevitable emergence of those who control but are not controlled. We see the power-drunk, possession-mad upper crust of the tycoon class, or members of a polit-bureau, lording it economically and socially over their inferiors, creating envy and strife. Decentralized, small communities cannot be organized into mob violence for political ends, or into merely violent demonstrating mobs, which are the end-product of frustration and failure to provide constructive and qualitatively satisfying occupation. Mindless work in large factories must inevitably produce mindless boredom and mindless violence.

As to non-violence and harmlessness, all the traditions of the world speak with one voice:

Taoism – 'Recompense injury with kindness'.
Confucianism – 'Do not to others what you would not wish done to yourself'.
Hinduism – 'If the injured return their injuries the consequences would be the destruction of every living creature and sin would prevail in the world'.
Buddhism – 'Be not wrath with those who are wrath with you and reply to harsh words with sweet'.
Jainism – 'Conquer wrath with forgiveness'.
Old Testament – 'A soft answer turneth away wrath'.
New Testament – 'Bless them that curse you, do good to them that hate you'.
Qur'an – 'To recompense evil conquer it with good'.

Taoism and Confucianism both say that the only really effective teaching is through example based on the perfection of the Sage who is so attuned to Nature that he cannot do wrong and is incapable of causing harm either to himself or anyone else. For the beginner, the asprirant to the Way, morals and ethics are still necessary as a guide to prevent him harming himself and others, and he must maintain the *yin-yang* balance and harmony as exemplified by the Sage. The wrong, the immoral, the 'sin' is that which disturbs this balance and affects first the individuals and then through them the whole world. One has every right to note the life-style of the preacher or teacher, not in the sense of criticism but as a pragmatic assessment of the value of his teaching. Again, 'that which we are, we shall teach, not voluntarily but involuntarily'.[2] If the 'master' cannot manage his own life and live in harmony he automatically disturbs everyone and everything around him, and so fails to offer an effective example for others to follow.

Extremes are to be avoided since they are incompatible with balance, putting undue weight on one side or the other, whether religious, political or moral. Extremes are the sphere of the essentially ignorant and immature. All militancy is a mistake; being an extreme measure, it involves 'excess of strength' in which 'there exists regret' and from which it is difficult to retreat in the event of going too far – flexibility and command of the situation are lost and over-balance and catastrophe become inevitable. All extremes contain a certain degree of the pathological, an emotional or mental excess and imbalance: they defeat their own ends in arousing strong opposition and in giving rise to fanaticism and bigotry. Taoism, Confucianism and Buddhism all preach the Doctrine of the Mean. It is a difficult path to tread. 'The knowing go beyond it, and the stupid do not come up to it', but 'the perfect man embodies the course of the Mean'. It is 'to show forbearance and gentleness in teaching others', and when 'the states of equilibrium and harmony exist in perfection, a happy order will prevail throughout heaven and earth and all things will be nourished and flourish'. But 'the path may not be left for an instant. If it could be left it would not be the path.'

Closely associated with the Doctrine of the Mean is the idea of *wu-wei*, non-interference, often translated as non-action, but possibly better called non-assertion. It is action without exertion in which nothing impedes the natural flow, nothing exceeds necessity. It is the absence of calculated activity, and instinctive and intuitive response to the present moment, the immediate situation. Any action which arises from self-motive projects its own force which must be actualised in both the present and the future. To overcome this action in the phenomenal world is to achieve *wu-wei*, 'actionless action'. Wisdom is inate and is only obscured by desires and opinions. Once the monkey-mind is stilled wisdom rises naturally to the surface; without action it acts. As Plotinus put it: 'Let go and let the Spirit flow in'. Or, from the *Bhagavad Gita:* 'One who is in union with the Divine and who knows the truth will maintain "I do not act at all".' In modern times, A. K. Coomaraswamy preaches the same doctrine: 'The work will be done the more easily and "skillfully" the less it is referred to our self and the more we let Him act through us. It is not idleness, but a facility that the "action without activity" of the *Bhagavad Gita* and the corresponding Taoist *wu-wei* intend.'[3]

Taoism is anti-activist; it laughs at people who think they

have all the answers and are engaged in organizing and manipulating others for their good, regardless of the fact that they do not necessarily know what that good is or what its consequences may be, even to the extent of producing actual evil in forcing people to conform against their wills or consciences, as with totalitarian states and unionism.

In his matchless style, Oscar Wilde castigates action: 'Don't talk about action. It is a blind thing dependent on external influences and moved by an impulse of whose nature it is unconscious. It is a thing incomplete in its essence, because limited by accident and ignorant of its direction, because always at variance with its aim. Its basis is the lack of imagination. It is the last resource of those who know not how to dream ... It dies at the moment of its energy. It is a base concession to fact. The world is made for the singer and dreamer.' Most action is interference and interference is, as Chuang Tzu says: 'like trying to stop an echo by shouting at it', and this is called *yu-wei*, useless effort. But not all effort is useless: 'Using boats on water, sledges on sand, sleighs on mud, or litters on mountain paths; digging channels for summer floods, arranging protection against winter cold ... such activities are not what may be called *yu-wei*. The Sages, in all their actions, follow the Nature of things.' Professor Needham maintains that *wu-wei* as action in accordance with Nature must be correlated with not-acting contrary to Nature, the very essence of Taoism; this too reflects the *yin-yang* aspects in balance.

5

THE YIN AND THE YANG
IN NATURE

Nowhere is the balance of the *yin* and the *yang* in Nature shown better than in the development of the typical Chinese garden, which was essentially Taoist in origin. The Han Emperors had earlier created vast artificial landscapes and parks with mountains, ravines, forests, rivers, lakes and open spaces to provide a habitat for hordes of game for hunting; but during the time of the Six Dynasties and the T'ang, when Taoism prevailed, there developed the quiet intimacy of the Taoist garden, intended to reflect heaven on earth. It became a symbol of Paradise where all life was protected and sheltered. The park had been given over to the grandiose, the artificial, extravagant and luxurious, to the hunter and aggressor; the Taoist garden was a place of naturalness and simplicity, a haven for Sage, scholar and nature lover as well as animal, bird and plant life.

Both landscape painting and garden-making owed their development to the Taoist philosophers who derived their inspiration from Nature as the Mother of All Things, the womb of life, eternal renewal, with all her rhythms and moods. What was said of the painting of a landscape applied equally to the creation of a garden; 'Chinese painters intuitively felt these same forces to be the visible, material manifestations of a higher all-embracing Reality; the Word made – not flesh – but Living Nature'. Or: 'The Sages cherish the Tao within them, while they respond to the objective world ... As to landscapes, they both have material existence and reach to the realms of the Spirit ... the virtuous follow the Tao by spiritual insight and the wise take the same approach. Landscapes capture the Tao by their forms and the virtuous take pleasure in them. Is this not almost the same thing? ... The Divine Spirit is infinite, yet it dwells in forms and inspires likeness and thus truth enters into forms and signs.'[2] But while landscapes portray the vastness and grandeur of Nature, the garden reveals the intimate aspect.

All forms of art are the outward and visible expression of *Ch'i*, the Cosmic breath or Energy, with which all creation must be in accord, whether it be painting, poetry, music or the creation of a garden. Indeed, all these arts are developed side by side, for the Chinese scholar was expected to be capable of interpreting the same inspiration in all three arts together and the place of both their inspiration and expression was most usually the garden, this term being applied also to the rural retreat of a Sage or hermit, where, in some remote and beautiful scenery, a hut had been built and round it trees planted. In a well-designed garden it should be difficult to distinguish between the work of man and Nature. One should 'borrow scenery from Nature' and the ideal place was 'among trees in the mountains'. Wherever it was, the garden was a place of quiet, meditation and communion with Nature, whether in wild scenery beside a waterfall, or a trickling stream, or in a bamboo grove, or courtyard of a city dwelling.

The garden is 'the natural home of man' and house and garden were situated according to *feng-shui* (wind and water) influences in harmony with the currents of *Ch'i*; these were held in balance in both house and garden, as in Nature, by the *yin-yang* force. The *yin* lunar and *yang* solar powers were represented by the *yin* valleys and waters and the *yang* mountains and sky with all their endless *yang* and *yin* qualities such as sunshine and shadow, height and depth, heat and cold.

However small the space utilized, the garden was never laid out as a flat expanse from which all could be viewed at once.

This removal of any definite boundary made for succession, expansion, rhythm and the sense of unlimited time and space. The garden, like Nature, is ever-changing, a place of light and shade with a life-breath *(Ch'i yün)* which is in harmony with the rhythms of the seasons and their contrasts in weather. Irregularity of line also suggests movement and life. 'Everything that is ruled and symmetrical is alien to free Nature.'[3] Or, as it has been said: 'The awareness of change, the interaction symbolized by the *yin-yang* theory, has caused Chinese gardeners to seek irregular and unexpected features which appeal more to the imagination than to the reasoning faculty of the beholder. There were certain rules and principles for gardening, but these did not lead to any conformity. The basic elements were the same as for landscape painting, *shan shui* or "mountain and water".'[4] This 'mountain and water' might be either imposing scenery or simply a pond and rocks. The smallest space could be converted into an effect of depth, infinite extension and mysterious distance; groves, rockeries, bushes, winding paths, all helped to lure on beyond the immediate scene. As Rowley says of Western and Chinese art: 'We restrict space to a single vista as though seen through an open door; they suggest the unlimited space of Nature as though they had stepped through that open door'.[5]

The entire garden must be considered in association and relationship with all things in Nature. Chang Ch'ao says: 'Planting flowers serves to invite butterflies, piling up rocks serves to invite the clouds, planting pine trees serves to invite the wind ... planting banana trees serves to invite the rain and planting willow trees serves to invite the cicada'. These are all traditionally symbolic associations.

In the past in China, though man was the mediator between Heaven and Earth, he was not the measure of the universe; his place was simply to maintain the balance and harmony between the *yin* and the *yang*. It was Nature which was the Whole, the controlling cosmic power. The garden helped man in his work of maintaining harmony; it also had an ethical significance and influence. According to Ch'ien Lung it had 'a refreshing effect upon the mind and regulated the feelings', preventing man from becoming 'engrossed in sensual pleasures and losing strength of will'. Its pleasures were simple, natural and spiritual. A Suchou poet wrote of the garden: 'One should enter it in a peaceful and receptive mood; one should use one's observation to note the plan and pattern of the garden, for the different parts have not been arbitrarily assembled, but carefully weighed against each other like the pairs of inscribed tablets placed in the pavilions,[6] and when one has thoroughly comprehended the tangible forms of objects one should endeavour to attain an inner communication with the soul of the garden and try to understand the mysterious forces governing the landscape and making it cohere.'

The garden was for all seasons with their changing moods and colours, flowers and trees; so the pavilion and open gallery were necessary for enjoyment in the heat of summer or the cold of winter and became an integral part of the scenery. Even in winter one sat in the pavilion to admire the beauties of the snow and watch the budding of the almond and plum blossom. A portable brazier of glowing charcoal kept one warm and a large brazier was used to melt the snow to make the tea. The garden was particularly evocative by moonlight, and the new and full moons, times of spiritual power, had their own festivals – especially the festival of the mid-autumn moon. Other festivals were also celebrated in the pavilion or garden; the vernal equinox, observed on the twelfth day of the second month of the Chinese year, was known as the Birthday of the Flowers.

Pavilions and galleries obviously had to blend with their surroundings. The *Yüan Yeh* says: 'Buildings should be placed so as to harmonize with the natural formation of the ground'. When pavilions were connected by galleries, these followed the rise and fall and curves of the land or winding of the waters which were often crossed by bridges, bringing in all the symbolism of the crossing of the waters, of transition, of communication between one realm or plane and another, as well as of man as mediator, occupying the central position between the great powers. Added beauty and symbolism was introduced in the 'moon bridge', a lovely half-circle which when reflected in the clear water below formed the perfect circle of the full moon.

Roofs were curved and painted and the lattice work of the balustrades was lacquered and painted in harmonizing and symbolic colours. Harmony and proportion had to be maintained, but symmetry was alien to Nature. Thus the

Figure 7. Moon bridge and pavilion.

...tained no such thing as clipped lawns or hedges or ...ically designed flower beds, or flowers marshalled ...tterns. Any 'landscaping' had to absorb buildings ...nted trees, make them look as if they had grown ...erects a pavilion where the view opens and plants ...t smile in the face of the spring breeze.'[7] It was a ...oth relaxation and active enjoyment, for solitary ...i and study or for convivial gatherings of friends to ...drink tea or wine or take *al fresco* meals. There they ...l poetry and music, painted, practised calligraphy or ...philosophy. One amusement was to compose a ...he time that it took a floating wine cup and saucer to ...i one end to the other on a meandering water-course ...e floor of the pavilion. A poet failing to complete his poem in the time had to catch and empty the cup. These water courses could also be constructed in symbolic forms such as the swastika, or the cross-form of the Chinese character for the number ten, or in the shape of a lotus or open flower. Sometimes the water tumbled over small waterfalls or rocks.

Pavilions were given names such as the Pavilion of the Hanging Rainbow, the Fragrance of the Lotus, the Secret Clouds, or the Eight Harmonious Tones, Invitation or Contemplation of the Moon, Welcoming Spring, Pleasant Coolness, and so on. In some gardens there were Halls of the Moon. These were constructed in the shape of a hemisphere, the vaulted ceiling painted to represent the nocturnal sky with innumerable small windows of coloured glass depicting the moon and stars. The total effect was one of subdued light like a summer's night. Sometimes the floor was planted with flowers, but more usually it contained running water, the moon and water being closely allied: 'The moon washes its soul in the clear waters'; but although moon and waters are both *yin*, water is also symbolically related to the sun since it catches and reflects back the sun's light, the *yang*. These halls could be large enough for holding banquets or of a smallness suitable for intimate sitting about in conversation or listening to poetry and music. Here, in the garden, where heaven and earth meet, music and poetry became the natural form for the expression of harmony.

While the pavilion was built in and for the garden and was open to it, this breaking down of the distinction between in

Figure 8. Pavilion and rock.

and out of doors applied also to the dwelling house which was not only sited for *feng-shui* but for fitting as naturally as possible into the scenery and giving access so immediately to the garden that there seemed no dividing line. Doors either did not exist or were left open. (Socially, closed doors were not considered courteous since they implied exclusion, while the open door symbolized the welcome extended by the essentially out-going Chinese temperament with its spontaneous and natural relationships developed over the ages in the highly socialized life of a large family or clan.) Doors were often only a means of enhancing a view into the garden or the scenery beyond, such as was the moon door, a beautifully placed circle framing some special outlook. Not only was every aspect used to its full natural advantage but 'if one can take advantage of a neighbour's view one should not cut off the communication, for such a "borrowed prospect" is very acceptable'.[8]

The house opened on to the garden and the garden came into the house; rooms opened on to the courtyards where flowering shrubs and trees grew and ferns and flowers fringed a central pool, usually with golden carp swimming in it, for the garden was a place for animal and bird life also. Indeed, animals and plants were not considered the only 'living' things; everything shares in the cosmic power and mountains and rivers also 'live'. Nor was it at all unusual for the house to go out into the garden, for the lover of Nature would move a bed out of doors, beside some special tree, shrub or flower which was coming into bloom, so that no stage of its development and beauty would be lost; or one would sit up all night to enjoy the effect of the moonlight. 'The moonlight lies like glittering water over the countryside. The wind sighs in the trees and gently touches the lute and the book that lie on the couch. The dark rippled mirror of the water swallows the half-moon. When day dawns one is awakened by the fresh breeze; it reaches the bed and all the dust of the world is blown out of one's mind.'[9]

The garden was not, however, merely aesthetic but creative and a reminder of, and contact with, the creative forces of the earth and the great cycle of the seasons, birth, maturity, decay, death and rebirth.

The merging of the native Taoism with imported Buddhism in Ch'an, or Zen, carried on the tradition of the intimate relationship between man and Nature. Ch'an Buddhism and gardens were two facets of Chinese inspiration which were adopted and carried on by the Japanese, but in later decadent times the original symbolism of the garden as a reflection of Paradise was lost and gardens became mere pleasure grounds, except where attached to monasteries, in which much of the symbolism was taken over and where the associations with meditation remained. In these gardens of the effete times artificial extravagances crept in; windows were made in shapes which bore no relation to symbols, such as teapots, animals, vases and fans, although some of these forms had, in fact, a symbolic content. But these aberrations were stigmatized by the *Yüan Yeh* as 'stupid and vulgar' and 'intelligent people should be careful in such matters'.

The garden was a reflection of the macrocosm and embodied all the *yin-yang* dualisms projected in manifestation. Mountains, valleys, rivers, lakes, were all represented. As Cheng Pan ch'iao said: 'The enjoyment of life should come from a view regarding the universe as a garden ... so that all beings live according to their nature and great indeed is such happiness'.

The importance of water in the Chinese garden was not only due to *yin-yang* symbolism but to the wide significance of water itself as, next to the Dragon, the greatest Taoist symbol. It is strength in weakness, fluidity, adaptability, coolness of judgement, gentle persuasion and passionlessness. While mountains and rocks are the bones of the body and the earth its flesh, rivers and streams are the arteries and blood, life giver and fertilizer. Flowing water and still water symbolized movement and repose, the complementary opposites, and water-worn stones symbolized the interaction of the soft and the hard. Still water also takes on all the symbolism of the mirror.

Water could be introduced by forming lakes and rivers in the earth excavated for making mountains, though mountains were most frequently represented by rocks, hollow and weather-worn, fretted out by the restless sea or the elements or formed from the strange shapes of petrified trees. These rocks were carefully selected for their colour, texture, grain and shape; some were upright and towering, others, larger at the top than at the base, gave the effect of disappearing into the clouds; others, lying down, took fantastic animal shapes, some gave out a note when struck, others were mute. Sometimes the rocks formed grottoes, but whatever the shape they always appeared as natural to the setting and were as near to the forms of wild mountain crags as possible, giving the impression of Nature, untamed and capricious. (In this 'naturalness' it must be remarked that the mountains of China in the Yangtse gorges, the far West and the southern provinces have been worked by Nature herself into fantastic and sometimes grotesque shapes.) 'Try to make your mountains resemble real mountains. Follow Nature's plan' but 'do not forget they have to be built by human hands'.[10]

Symbolically, the mountain is, of course, the world axis, but in the Chinese garden it also represented the *yang* power in Nature with the waters as the *yin*. The 'mountain' is traditionally placed in the middle of a lake or pond, the rock being the stable and eternal, the water the flowing and temporal. This mountain-and-water *(shan shui)* symbolism also obtains in landscape painting. The rock and the shadow it casts are also *yang* and *yin*. Rocks are 'silent, unmovable and detached from life, like refined scholars'. Their ruggedness also suggests the challenging and dangerous element in the mountains and life.

In larger gardens the mountains were sufficiently high for the formation of small valleys and dales, with winding streams opening out into lakes on which boat journeys could be taken and where water could be spanned by bridges. Sometimes a series of islands or rocks were so connected. Tunnels in the rocks gave the same effect and carried the same symbolism as bridges in passing from one world to another. But 'even a little mountain may give rise to many effects ... a small stone may evoke many feelings'.[11] Shen Fu says: 'In the designing of a rockery or the training of flowering trees one should try to show the small in the large and the large in the small and provide for the real in the unreal and the unreal in the real. One reveals and conceals alternately, making it sometimes apparent and sometimes hidden'.

Both the *yang* mountain and the *yin* tree are axial and so represent stability and balance between the two Great Powers; they also offer a line of communication for man between the celestial *yang* forces coming down to earth and to earthly *yin* forces reaching up to heaven, with man again as central and responsible for the maintenance of balance and harmony in responding equally to both powers.

Trees were an essential feature of both the domestic and hermitage garden, particularly the latter where they were often the only addition made by man to the natural scenery; their variety was almost as important as the trees themselves. While all trees are beautiful and symbolize the feminine power, some were especially noted for their *yin-yang* qualities. Though *yin* as a tree, the pine and cedar express *yang* masculine dignity and rigidity in contrast to the feminine gracefulness, pliability and charm of the willow, both these trees were considered necessary for the maintenance of the *yin-yang* harmony. Flowering trees such as the almond, cherry, plum and peach were esteemed – one should say loved – for their beauty and their symbolism. The almond, as the first flower of the year, is in many traditions the Awakener, watchfulness. Flowering in winter it is also courage in adversity. The cherry depicts delicacy of feeling and purity on the *yin* side and nobility on the *yang*. The plum, a symbol of winter and beauty, also signified strength, longevity and the hermit; it is one of the favourite subjects for artists. The plum, pine and bamboo were called 'the three friends of winter'. The almond and plum are both symbolic of new life coming in spring, but the plum should have a gnarled trunk and branches, called 'sleeping dragons', as the *yang* aspect, to offset the delicate blossoms of the *yin*; they also represent the old and the new together. Just as lovers of the garden would move their beds out under trees, so we read of artists who wandered all night in the moonlight to catch every phase of the beauty of 'the dry limbs clad in jade-white blooms'.

The peach holds a special position as the tree of the Taoist genii or Immortals; it is the Tree of Life at the centre of Paradise. It is also the Tree of Immortality and one bite of the fruit growing on the tree confers immediate immortality. Peach stones were apotropaic and were beautifully and symbolically carved and kept, or worn, as amulets and talismans. The tree is a symbol of spring, youth, marriage, wealth and longevity.

Pre-eminent among flowers were the lotus, peony and chrysanthemum. The peony is the only purely *yang* flower. Flowers, with their cup shape, naturally depict the *yin* receptive aspect in nature, but the peony is a royal flower, flaunting the red, fiery, masculine colour; it is also nobility, glory, riches. The chrysanthemum, on the other hand, is a flower of quiet retirement, the beloved flower of the cultured scholar, the retired official, who was, of course, also a scholar, and of the philosopher and poet. It was so much cultivated in retirement that it became a symbol of that life and of leisure. It signifies longevity, as being that which survives the cold, and as autumnal it is harvest and wealth, but it is primarily ease, leisure, joviality and enjoyment. Yüan Chung-lang said that the retired and the scholar were fortunate in having 'the enjoyment of the hills and water, flowers and bamboo' largely to themselves since 'luckily they lie outside the scope of the strugglers for fame and power who are so busy with their engrossing pursuits that they have no time for enjoyment'.

But the lotus, a universal symbol in the East (its symbolism is taken on by the lily and sometimes the rose in the West), is 'the flower that was in the Beginning, the glorious lily of the Great Waters ... that wherein existence comes to be and passes away'. It is both *yin* and *yang* and contains within itself the balance of the Two Powers; it is solar, as blooming in the sun, and lunar, as rising from the dark of the waters of pre-cosmic chaos. As the combination of air and water, this symbolizes spirit and matter. Its roots, bedded in the darkness of the mud, depict indissolubility; its stem, the umbilical cord of life, attaches man to his origins and is also a world axis; rising through the opaque waters of the manifest world, the leaves and flowers reach and unfold in the air and sunlight, typifying potentiality in the bud and spiritual expansion and realization in the flower; its seeds, moving on the waters, are creation. The lotus is associated with the wheel both as the solar matrix and the sun-wheel of cycles of existence. Iamblicus calls it perfection since its leaves, flowers and fruit form the circle. As lunar-solar, *yin-yang*, the lotus is also the androgyne, the self-existent. It has an inexhaustible symbolism in Hinduism, Taoism and Buddhism alike. Again it appears as both solar and lunar associated with sun gods such as Surya and lunar goddesses such as Lakshimi; solar with Amitaba and lunar with Kwan-yin and androgynous in Kwannon. The lotus is the Golden Flower of Taoism, the crystalization and experience of light, the Tao. While on the spiritual level it represents the whole of birth, growth, development and potentiality, on the mundane plane

it depicts the scholar-gentleman who comes in contact with
the mud and dirty water of the world but is uncontaminated
by it. Apart from its almost endless symbolism, the lotus is a
flower of great beauty and highly evocative; as Osvald Sirén
says, a sheet of lotus blossom 'emanates a peculiar magic, an
atmosphere that intoxicates like fragrant incense and lulls like
the rhythm of a rising and falling mantra'.[12]

Ancient China understood many things which are only now
reaching the West and being hailed as new discoveries. She
anticipated by centuries the 'discovery' that flowers and plants
have feelings. Yüan Chung-lang knew that they have their likes
and dislikes and compatibilities among other vegetation and
that they respond to care and appreciation in more than a
material way. The flowers in a Chinese garden were genuinely
loved, not in any 'precious' aestheticism, but rather in an
intimate relationship between living individuals. He said that
'flowers have their moods of happiness and sorrow and their
time of sleep ... when they seem drunk, or quiet and tired and
when the day is misty, that is the sorrowful mood of flowers ...
when they bask in the sunlight and their delicate bodies are
protected from the wind, that is the happy mood of flowers.
... When the ancient people knew a flower was about to bud
they would move their beds and pillows and sleep under it
watching how the flower passed from infancy to maturity and
finally dropped off and died ... As for all forms of noisy
behaviour and common vulgar prattle, they are an insult to the
spirits of flowers. One should rather sit dumb like a fool than
offend them.'[13] Among things which flowers dislike are: too
many guests; ugly women putting flowers in their hair; dogs
fighting; writing poems by consulting a rhyming dictionary;
books kept in bad condition; spurious paintings and common
monks talking Zen! On the other hand they do like a visiting
monk who understands tea!

Picked flowers and vases of flowers should never be
regarded as normal, only as a temporary expedient employed
by those living in cities and unnatural places deprived of hills
and lakes or any garden.

For the town-dweller or for one kept indoors of necessity,
the miniature garden was created. Though it was also seen in
pavilions, it was most usually on the tables of scholars. It, too,
symbolized Paradise, the Isles of the Blessed or the Abode of

the Immortals reflected in miniature perfection with the whole range of the *yin-yang* symbolism. Exceptionally beautiful stones and shells were used and there were miniature grottoes, trees, bamboos and grasses growing among the mountains, valleys and waters. The making of these gardens was an art in itself; just as Wang Wei maintained that the artist can bring Nature into the space of a small painting, so the creator of a garden, large or small or miniature, can concentrate the cosmos within its bounds.

Enclosing the whole garden in the city, or where the extent of the ground was limited, was the wall which was used not only as a boundary but as a setting for trees, shrubs and flowers; it could also provide an aperture which opened on to some special view. In the city, where space was restricted, walls were often a garden in themselves, sometimes built with considerable width, giving a roof-garden effect, or with trees and shrubs planted on top and ferns in the crevices below. Enclosing walls also helped to make the city garden a place where one could find 'stillness in turmoil'. Apart from the symbolism of the enclosed garden as Paradise, the walls brought in the *yin-yang* significance of the interplay of light and shade.

Unfortunately China now joins the industrial nations of the world in exploiting Nature. Hideous concrete blocks of flats, offices and factories insulate man from any contact with the yellow earth and even in the country, in the 'communes', ugly blocks of dwelling houses and buildings scar the landscape and violate all traditional rules. Sadly, Seyyed Hossein Nasr's words can be applied: 'There is nearly total disequilibrium between modern man and Nature as attested in nearly every expression of modern civilization which seeks to offer a challenge to nature rather than co-operate with it ... the harmony between man and nature has been destroyed'.[14] The *yin-yang* balance and harmony has been betrayed.

6

THE I CHING:
THE BOOK OF CHANGES

As has been said, Confucius regarded the *I Ching* as so important that he wrote ten commentaries on it and said that if he had another life he would spend it entirely on the Book of Changes.

The work begins with the *T'ai Ch'i*, Primordial Unity, which, descending into the world of duality as the 'Two Determinants', the *yin* and the *yang*, female and male, produced the Four Designs, which gave rise to the Eight Diagrams, the *Pa Kua*. This interaction of the *yin-yang* powers, or energies, is responsible for the whole phenomenal world. Neither power is complete in itself, nor can it stand alone, but in combination and co-operation they give rise to all forms and existence in Nature. The two forces have absolute equality and balance of power. Their interaction produces the Five Elements which are formed from the primordial substance and it is from them that the manifest world becomes differentiated and is brought into being.

The *I Ching* is an interpretation of cosmic phenomena and their interrelatedness, but it also provides a manual for human conduct in relationship to the powers of the universe. It is used by Taoist and Confucianist alike. It might also be said to constitute a certain mysticism of numbers, such as appeared later with the Pythagoreans and Neo-Platonists. In it, the sequence of hexagrams symbolizes and makes intelligible the polarity in Nature and in the everyday life in the world. After the first bare statements of the *yang* and the *yin*, the creative and the receptive, energy and inertia, each condition leads inevitably to its opposite and requires balance between the two: *T'ai*, Peace, leads to *P'i* standstill. The alternating hexagrams illustrate the laws of balance, compensation and reconciliation, so that, as said, each trigram and hexagram is associated with its complementary and opposite quality, the two being inseparable, unable to exist except in relationship.

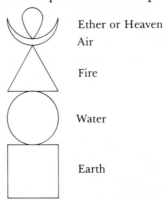

Ether or Heaven
Air

Fire

Water

Earth

Figure 9. The Five Elements in Stupa form.

When the same combination of two trigrams is inverted a warning is given, as when, for example, the hexagram 14, *Ta Yu*, Great Possessions, is followed by 15, *Ch'ien*, Modesty and Humility, which are necessary to balance and harmony in such circumstances; fortune may easily turn to misfortune, while that which appears unfortunate at the time may carry the germs or means of future fortune. Even one line can contain both the opposites of fortune and misfortune, as in the hexagram 13, *T'ung Jen*, where the fifth place says: 'Men bound in fellowship first weep, but afterwards they laugh'; or, again: 'War is both a poison and a medicine'. Thus 'the wise man maintains an even course through prosperity and adversity and is neither elated by the one nor downcast by the other'. This is the cyclic movement which obtains throughout the manifest world until the motionless Centre is reached, it being the place from which movement originates and to which it returns. The nearer the state of perfection the more delicate the balance; on a broad plane, balance is relatively easy; on a pinnacle it becomes precarious and demanding. The strong all *yang* line in a hexagram –0– (3 + 3 + 3) overbalances and becomes a line of motion; it is over-positive, just as the all *yin* line –X– (2 + 2 + 2) is completely negative, and both being over-loaded must lead to a situation of change. The top-heavy falls over and becomes its opposite; having been in the ascending *yang* and reaching the top of the hill it can go no further and can therefore only descend into the valley, the *yin*. Nothing can remain static. In the *I Ching* this is illustrated by the static numbers 7 and 8, where the *yang* odd number 7 is made up of 2 + 2 + 3, that is, a preponderence of the even number of *yin*, and the *yin* even number 8 is composed of 3 + 3 + 2, a preponderence of *yang*. *Yang* numbers are forward movement, *yin* represents backward movement; but whichever way they move they come to the same result and add to the same totality:

$$\left. \begin{array}{l} \textit{Yang } 7 \\ \textit{Yin } \ \ 8 \end{array} \right\} = 15 \qquad\qquad \left. \begin{array}{l} -9 \\ 6- \end{array} \right\} = 15$$

The trigrams are expanded into hexagrams because as trigrams alone they merely represent ideas, states, or things, whereas the development into hexagrams introduces relationships and the interplay of these ideas, states, or things and their reactions on one another, symbolizing, in fact, the interplay of the whole manifest world in its powers of attraction and repulsion.

The hexagrams also represent endlessly continuing life-force, one form giving way and giving rise to its opposite, life to death, death to life, an eternal cyclic transformation. They also symbolize all possibilities, both personal and collective, in the universe. This is also depicted in the *yin-yang* construction of the trigrams for the opposites, fire and water, ☲ ☵ the two great creative-destructive forces in the world, responsible for life and death. The most obvious illustration of the cyclic is the passage of the seasons with their birth, growth, maturity and death; but, as Emerson says: 'Every ultimate fact is only the first of a new series; every general law only a particular fact of some more general law presently to disclose itself'.

With the cosmos viewed as in a state of flux there can be nothing static or totally self-contained; every thing, every entity, acts on and conditions every other. Opposites do not exclude each other but show themselves as different aspects of the whole. Change is a dynamic force working from within.

It is in constant change and growth alone that life can be grasped at all. If it is interrupted the result is not death, which is only an aspect of life, but life's reversal, its perversion. This perception is highly characteristic of the Chinese concept of change. The opposite of change is neither rest nor standstill, for these are aspects of change. The idea that the opposite of change is regression and not cessation of movement, brings out clearly the contrast with our category of time. The opposite of change in Chinese thought is the growth of what ought to decrease, the downfall of what ought to rule. Change, then, is not simply movement as such, for its opposite is also movement. Change is natural movement, rather, development that can only reverse itself by going against nature.[1]

Heraclitus, a Nature-lover and a solitary, saw everything as in flux, and change prevailing in the whole universe; for him the law of polarity was the supreme principle of the cosmos, but he saw the opposites as in conflict, that they must clash, and he maintained that friction, the centrifugal and centripetal forces, were necessary for life as the spur of opposition. Strength is gained by opposition and overcoming obstacles. He accused Homer of praying for the destruction of the universe when he asked that strife might perish from among the gods and men as then everything would come to an end, though he agreed with Plato that the ultimate reality is both the Many and the One and that the conflicting powers must ultimately be harmonized in the Logos. The Heraclitian opposition differs from the Two Powers of Taoism in that the latter are not in conflict with each other but exist in complementary tension. The Heraclitian flux is lawless, although Heraclitus allows for certain laws in the world, whereas in Taoism the Tao is responsible for order in the universe, an order to which man must conform to maintain

Figure 10. **Imperial mourning robe showing the *yin* and *yang*** contending dragons, symbolizing polarity in the universe.

balance and harmony. Although change is a symptom of inherent imperfection, the process of change is a controlled and orderly one, neither haphazard nor a matter of chance. All manifestation is finite and imperfect and in a state of perpetual flux; only the Tao is unchanging and everlasting, although even the word 'everlasting' falls short of the true meaning since the Tao is beyond time. The Tao is all-inclusive, hence change must also be within it and there is then an element of constancy in change. The vital force *Ch'i* condenses and dissolves in perpetual change, alternating between the *yin* and the *yang* in endless relationship, interplay and harmony, a constant flow of energy passing between them in the cosmos. Philosophy and science both assume law and order in daily life, expecting to find the unvarying progression of sunrise and sunset, days, years and seasons, and all change is contained within these rules; change and order go hand-in-hand. As the Buddha said, change is not the same as chaos and it is in no sense a matter of caprice, but maintains its own order and laws just as a tree, growing from seed to sapling to massive size changes beyond recognition but still maintains its tree-nature. Radhakrishnan says: 'Life is no thing or state of thing but a continuous movement of change'.[2] Hegel expresses it as: 'Inasmuch as the "state or condition" is cancelled through change, change itself also is cancelled'.

All things are together in action,
But I look into their non-action,
For things are continually moving, restless,
Yet all is proceeding back to its origin.
Proceeding back to the origin means quietness,
To be in quietness is to see 'being-for-itself.'
'Being-for-itself' is the all-changing-changeless.
To understand the all-changing-changeless is to be
enlightened.[3]

To be enlightened is to attain the perfect spontaneity of the Sage who, as Xenophanes puts it, 'effortlessly sets all things astir by the power of his mind alone'. This is perfectly exemplified in Lao Tzu and Chuang Tzu, the former terse, enigmatic and challenging, the latter the poet-philosopher mystic, flexible, flowing, brilliant and humorous, both in accord with the natural, the Tao, so that their teaching rises spontaneously, has the effortlessness of *wu-wei* and brings the spiritual down to earth and raises earth to heaven.

This spontaneity is also the 'play' of the universe so beautifully symbolized in Eastern religions, particularly Hinduism, as the divine creative dance which is the most significant illustration of the oneness of the universe, since at no point can the dance and the dancer be separated; the creative force in the cosmos cannot be dissociated from its creation. Shiva performs both the dance of creation and destruction. When he dances with a woman the dance is gentle, graceful and naturally creative, the *yin* and the *yang* are in balance; but when he dances alone it takes on the symbolism of the solitary, the ascetic, and becomes violent and destructive and the balance is lost.

Dervishes dancing portray the whirling and axial movement of the universe, its folding and unfolding, contraction and expansion, creation and dissolution, and bring the Supreme Essence into the realm of matter then return it back to the source from which it came. This, also, is perfect *yin-yang* symbolism, with the Essence as the Tao.

Dance-play both expresses and impresses significant experience; it expresses to the outward and visible world the symbolism of the movements, then impresses it on the inner mental and spiritual world.

Lyall Watson says:

Dancing must be the most basic and relevant of all forms of expression. Nothing can so effectively give outward form to an inner experience. Poetry and music exist in time. Painting and architecture are a part of space. But only the dance lives at once in both space and time. In it the creation and the thing created, the artist and the expression, are still one and the same thing. There is complete participation. There could be no better metaphor for an understanding of the mechanics of the cosmos ... We begin to realize that our universe is in a sense brought into being by the participation of those involved in it. It is a dance, for the vital ingredient is the act of participation.[4]

The same idea is expressed by Fritjof Capra in *The Tao of Physics:* 'Modern physics has shown us that movement and rhythm are essential properties of matter; that all matter, whether here on Earth or in outer space, is involved in a continuous cosmic dance. Eastern mystics have a dynamic view of the universe similar to that of modern physics.' He also says that it uses such phrases as 'the dance of creation and destruction' and 'energy dance'.

7

AWARENESS

'If your mind were free from formation and conception, how could illusions occur? When illusions do not occur, the real mind will be free to be aware of everything.' So said Tao-shin, the Fourth Patriarch, and this is only another way of expressing the Buddhist prescription 'only cease to cherish opinion' as a means of attaining awareness and enlightenment. But before awareness and identity can be achieved there is the dualism of the ego and the witness, the perceived and the perceiver, to be overcome. At first it is necessary to watch the thoughts, actions and reactions of the 'monkey-mind' of the ego, with its eternal operation of conflicting forces, its multiple 'I's; but when these are noted, unrepressed and accepted, insight is gained into their true meaning – or meaninglessness – and the watcher and the watched cease to have separate and opposed existences. As the 'fall' into the separate and self-conscious is the fruit of the Tree of Knowledge, so the journey back, through awareness, is to unity, the Absolute, the fruit of the Tree of Life.

In the early stages, looking at any thing, person or situation, sets up an immediate process of assessing, deducing and inferring from already accepted premises and prejudices which fit previous experiences and conclusions: everything is put into pigeon-holes, likening this to that, and assuming given results must follow – all of which is merely personal opinion which may be right or totally erroneous. Even though these opinions may be held by groups of people they are still related to the temperaments, social backgrounds and limitations of each individual in the group. Awareness is an impersonal state, devoid of expectancy for that which is coming and untainted by that which is past; the present moment is allowed to unfold itself and give full attention to the thing-as-it-is. Awareness is direct experience, not thinking 'about' a thing or naming it and so relegating it to the second-hand. The subjective and objective are both states in the dualistic, relative world. Complete awareness transcends them. 'Direct experience and awareness of direct experience constitute the whole problem.'[1] It is, in a sense, abandonment, it is to abandon preconceived notions, beliefs and associations, ego-orientation, set mental processes and 'schools of thought'; it is ceasing to strive and thus becoming free from tensions, letting things come naturally, seeing them dispassionately. It is an inward and natural response, not an observation from an outside viewpoint; it should be so much part of life and so spontaneous that it is not observed as such. To think 'I am writing these words' is to come outside the experience; while completely absorbed no thought of the function or the result intrudes. To say 'I find this scenery beautiful' is already to be separate from it; absorbed in its beauty I am unconscious of myself as a separate entity, I am one with it and 'I' cease to exist. Awareness brings a quality of both spontaneity and simultaneousness, it is the 'natural' response to the world around, to all life, to the seasons and all the cyclic and rhythmic process of being and becoming. Awareness 'responds silently to all conditions, yet it is attached to none of them'.[2] Or, as expressed in the West by Wordsworth, it is: 'that wise passiveness and fruitful equilibrium in which the soul sees into the heart of things'.

Awareness dissolves all extremes. Wu Men, who lived at Hangchow and died in 1260, said in his *Wu Men Kuan:* 'One must ripen slowly. One day inner and outer will be found to be one and you will wake up'. This is in line with all religious teaching that the unregenerate man is also the unawakened – expressed in 'awake thou that sleepest'. Awareness is wakefulness; a mental and spiritual immediacy. It also implies a delight in life, light-heartedness and lightness of touch; heaviness always impedes. This awakening is also liberation from the bondage of the illusory nature of the manifest world; it is to find 'emptiness', the Void, *Sunyata*, which is beyond conceptual thought and can only be realized by going through the levels of phenomenal and relative truths to get beyond them. The Void is not nihilism, on the contrary it expresses the Ultimate Reality which is beyond duality but is yet immanent in all things. 'When you hear me speak about the Void, do not fall into the idea that I mean vacuity.'[3] Huang-po also says: 'The sun rises and shines all over the world, but it does not light the Void; when the sun sets darkness comes to the world, but the Void is not darkened'. And Tao-shin, the Fourth Patriarch states: 'Void and being are not concerned as two. This is called the Middle Way. The Middle Way cannot be expressed in words.' The Middle Way is more than a path between extremes, it transcends them and unifies them in the Void. 'When discrimination is done away with, the Middle Way or *Sunyata* is reached.'

Emptiness is not synonymous with non-existence. 'The Voidness of the universe is capable of containing all things.'[4] The Void is the formless which gives rise to all forms in manifestation. For Taoism it is that from which all emerges and to which all returns; it is the Pleroma, a fullness rather than an 'emptiness' in the usually accepted sense; it is the Potential, the ultimate completion.

To attain enlightenment, the awakening, it is necessary to surpass the rational mind. The rational is derivative as opposed to intuitive and direct awareness; the rational divides the knower and the known, the intuitive suffers no such separation. The one is transmitted, the other grows naturally of itself if allowed to do so either in gradual or sudden enlightenment. Reason is necessary and valid in its own sphere, but is not capable of ultimate sufficiency, it cannot meet all human needs and must, therefore, be transcended after a certain stage has been reached through a power of immediate perception. The opposite of the rational is not necessarily the irrational but that which goes beyond logic and objective reasoning and includes the whole of man's potentialities and being which must, of course, include the rational before surpassing and superceding it.

Logic and reason treat everything as either/or, again, valid in their own spheres, but the direction they take is determined by the premises from which they start. Einstein maintained that 'Pure logical thinking cannot yield any knowledge of the empirical world; all knowledge of reality starts from experience and ends in it. Propositions arrived at by purely logical means are completely empty.' Eastern philosophy is largely concerned with finding means of surpassing, or of liberation from, the rational mind, concerned only with the relative and phenomenal world, and in gaining intuitive, spontaneous experience of 'suchness','the thing-in-itself', 'seeing into the true nature' concealed behind the facade of manifestation. Western philosophy, on the other hand, is largely speculative and is not related to any particular religious tradition; it can exist mentally without any relationship to a spiritual path, it can be associated with a religion, or none, and no spiritual discipline is required in its pursuit. Oriental religions and philosophies are not a formal or purely intellectual exercise, they take it for granted that they must influence and alter the whole being, they are a way of life, not a search for abstract ideas or logical justification for certain premises. Philosophical speculation, theological dogmas, arguments for and against the existence of God, or immortality, belong to the mental world and can easily become divorced from both the spiritual and everyday life. It is much more important to find the answer to the question 'Who am I?' and to find the meaning of being in this world; in other words to engage in the search for the encounter with the Self.

After the over-rationalization of the last century it is necessary to recognize what Professor Dodds writes of as being 'deeply and imaginatively aware of the power, the wonder and the peril of the Irrational ... in the Hellenistic Age too many of them made the fatal mistake of thinking they could ignore it. Modern man, on the other hand, is beginning to acquire such an instrument. It is still very far from perfect, nor is it always skillfully handled.'[5] The same criticism, pointing out the lack of imaginative awareness, is made of physical science by Arthur Ford, who says: 'Physical science has a great deal of know-how, but very little know-what or know-why. In analyzing a note it loses a symphony; in studying an atom it misses a universe. As a result it spurs us to do with greater efficiency things that never should have been done in the first place.'[6]

Taoism is existential in the sense that reality can only be lived and entered into, theory and speculation being second-hand; but it is also essential in that the Tao is the very essence to which this existence should lead. The existential nature of Taoism is not to be confused with modern abstract existential-ism, which is concerned with the petty ego, the self. Taoism is concerned with the nature of things as they are, with the supra-personal, the Self. Living experience is the point of departure. The Taoist hermit did not opt out of life, he opted in, into Nature, into the meaning of things. All he abandoned was artificiality in favour of simplicity. No one provided him with the means of living; he found his own. No one gave him 'social security'; he laughed at the very notion of security anyway, knowing there was no such thing. It is senseless to talk seriously of security; there is not, and never has been, any such thing. A glance at world history, or one small private life, is enough to dispel any such illusion. 'In Nature every moment is new; the past is always swallowed and forgotten; the coming only is sacred. Nothing is secure but life, transition and the energising spirit... people wish to be settled; only as far as they are unsettled is there any hope for them ... The way of life is wonderful; it is by abandonment.'[7]

The hermit and sage left the world in order to live in close contact with Nature, as Professor Needham puts it, they felt 'that human society could not be brought into order, as the Confucians strove to bring it, without a far greater knowledge and understanding of Nature outside and beyond human society... Confucian knowledge was masculine and managing; the Taoists condemned it and sought after a feminine and receptive knowledge which could arise only as the fruit of a passive and yielding attitude to the observation of Nature'.[8] Living in accord with Nature controlled the development of science and checked its unacceptable and unnatural aspects. Today the materialist looks at Nature with a view to what can be got out of her, how much she can be dominated and exploited. This power-craving is an immature and barbaric characteristic. The greater the civilization or individual mind the less it seeks to dominate either Nature or its fellow men. Now a maximum demand is made upon everything and the

Figure 11. The Great Dragon Screen in the Palace gardens at Pekin, showing the nine *yang* dragons and at the end the *yin* waters.

grotesque word 'maximize' has crept into the vocabulary of these get-the-most-out-of-it people who are exhausting Nature and the environment. This is also seen in the 'maximizing' of so-called needs far beyond the natural, indeed, most of them artificial in the extreme. One might quote E.F. Schumacher: 'The cultivation and expansion of needs is the antithesis of wisdom. It is also the antithesis of freedom and peace. Every increase of needs tends to increase one's dependence on outside forces, over which one cannot have control, and therefore increase existential fear. Only by a reduction of needs can one promote a genuine reduction of those which are the ultimate causes of strife and war.'[9]

People, when divorced from Nature, are dominated by the individual, self-centred and self-seeking ego; they feel alone and adrift in a hostile world and in consequence their reactions are hostile and either inwardly or overtly violent. Either they torture themselves with negative feelings of envy, resentment and hatred, or they lash out at society in violent political creeds, strikes or infuriated revolt. They have no conception of the ultimate unity of all life and are too blind to see that in hurting others they must hurt themselves, that disruption is a futile and childish reaction. On the other hand, those aware of their true nature create instead of destroy and are conscious not only of being part of a whole but also of being whole in themselves, which inevitably gives a profound respect for all life, an awareness of the meaning of existence and the value of every experience or thing encountered, so that instead of demanding more material possessions they are concerned rather with learning and experiencing more and hence naturally giving more. Any fool can destroy, and most fools do, but only the mind aware of things in themselves, of the oneness of life, can learn wisdom and become creative, can 'become what one is', in Buddhist phraseology, feel one with life and lose the sense of isolation and its consequent physical, mental and spiritual ills.

8

THE RESOLVING THIRD

Although the Tao is the One, the Absolute, the Formless, it has
different aspects in manifestation, these are inevitably three in
number: the Tao of Heaven, *T'ien Tao*; the Tao of Man, *Jen Tao*;
the Tao of Earth, *T'i Tao*, man occupying the middle and
mediating position. There was also a triad of gods in later
popular Taoism: *T'ai I*, the Grand Unity; *T'ien I*, the Heavenly
Unity and *T'i I*, the Earthly Unity. This Triad was at the head of
the hierarchy of spiritual beings, but the *T'ai I* represented the
supreme and final Unity. These 'gods' are aspects of life and
experience and, as powers, they are valid influences. The
monotheistic religions largely ignore these forces, but attribute
definite and finite qualities to God: God is Love, God is
Merciful, and so on; but the non-theistic religions, Taoism
and Buddhism, avoid all mention of a God as being beyond
definition or expression. Hinduism, although theistic, also
puts the Absolute, It, beyond all qualities and if referred to
employs the terms Brahman and Atman which, like the Tao
are untranslatable. Form creates relativity; the Tao, Atman,
can only be the Formless. The formal world is based on
relationship, cause and effect, time and space; not one of the
Ten Thousand Things stands by itself, there is no such thing as
an independent existence. Eckhart asks: 'When is a man in

mere understanding? I answer, when he sees one thing separate from another. And when is a man above understanding? That I can tell you: when a man sees All in all, then a man stands beyond mere understanding.'

All duality and polarity calls for a resolving third, which is on a plane above the opposites and acts as a catalyst, bringing about a state of equilibrium between the extremes. Yen Fu said: 'Tao is Primordial; it is Absolute. In its descent it begets one. When one is begotten, Tao becomes relative and two comes into existence. When two things are compared there is their opposite and three is begotten.' In the *Tao Te Ching* this is expressed as: 'All things are backed by Shade *(yin)* and faced by the Light *(yang)* and harmonized by the immaterial Breath *(ch'i)*'.

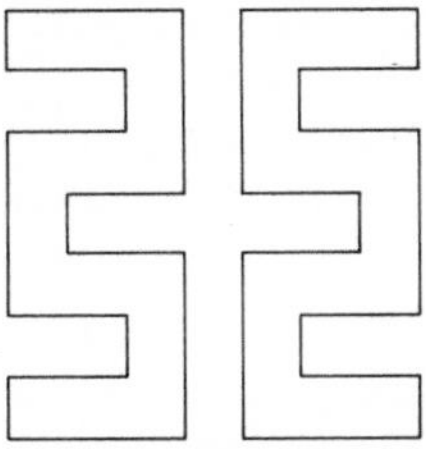

Figure 12. Ch'i, in the form of the *yin* and the *yang.*

Ordinary mind views everything as dualistic, subject and object, male and female, good and evil, but is ever striving to attain a state beyond in which duality is reconciled and lost in unity. In ancient Hinduism and Buddhism this was expressed by a Triad of male, female and the androgyne; the *sat-cit-ananda* of Hinduism is a triad of being, consciousness and bliss, with being and consciousness as common, in some degree, to all mankind, but needing the resolving third of divine bliss to lift them out of the mundane. The whole man involves intellect, emotion and will, a trinity. In the Hindu paths these are *jhana, bhakti* and *karma* yoga. In modern philosophy McTaggart puts the reconciling principle between will and intellect as love, maintaining that will and intellect are often in conflict until reconciled by love. For the Neo-Platonist Proclus, the Universal Mind unfolds itself in a triadic scheme of thesis, antithesis and synthesis, a system later adopted by Hegel and Fichte.

If there were no relationship there could be no give and take and all would be static and where relationship exists in duality it requires the reconciling third to rescue the two powers from eternal tension; the interplay and interaction of the third ensures ultimate completion. Of thesis, antithesis and synthesis, Coventry Patmore writes: 'Nature goes on giving echoes of the same living triplicity in animal, plant and mineral, every stone and material atom owing its being to the synthesis or 'embrace' of the two opposed forces of expansion and contraction. Nothing whatever exists in a single entity but in virtue of being thesis, antithesis and synthesis and in humanity and natural life this takes the form of sex, the masculine, feminine and neuter, or third forgotten sex spoken of by Plato, which is not the absence of the life of sex but its fulfilment and power as the electric fire is the fulfilment and power of positive and negative in their 'embrace'.'

In the symbolism of the tree and pillar, the two parallel trees or pillars represent the polar forces of the universe, the pairs of opposites, which face each other, giving and receiving; they are also the upward and downward in movement, tension and release, space and time, a symbolism which occurs in all religions. In Taoism and Confucianism it is, of course, the *yin* and *yang*; in Christianity it represents the dual nature of Christ. Mithraism depicts it as the dadophori. The two pillars of Solomon's Temple were Boaz and Jachin, the active and passive principles. When a third tree or pillar is introduced, or the branches of the tree meet and intertwine, we have a symbol of the resolving third and the return from dualism to unity. Dante wrote of three trees, the Left and Right Hand as the duad and the third as the Trinity.

In Alchemy the two forces are the male Sulphur and the female Quicksilver while Salt represents the unifying Spirit; they are the three of body, soul and spirit of male and female dissolved in the crucible, by fire, the *solve et coagula*, to become the Androgyne. This coincidence of opposites is always an inner movement, symbolically within the transforming vessel, the inner self.

Both Taoism and Buddhism employ paradox to avoid the sharp duality of the either/or limitations. Paradox and ambivalence are part of a deliberate avoidance of positive definition; that which is sharply defined is also limited and leaves no room for expansion or for the alternative possibilities expressed by paradox, just as the Taoist painting leaves space and suggests rather than defines and a Chinese poem does not multiply words or employ long descriptions but, like Taoist painting, leaves empty space to draw one into participation and leave room for the imagination.

Seemingly contradictory statements can both be true at different levels of understanding; to the senses the world is real, in *advaita* it is unreal. There are degrees of reality, each true at a particular level of experience. Inexactness and inconsistence are qualities inherent in anything in a state of flux, the ever-shifting sands of the phenomenal world, until all is reconciled in the ultimate Oneness. Into this philosophy of Both comes also that of Neither/Nor, well illustrated in the Upanishads by the statement that neither ignorance nor knowledge is acceptable. 'In dense darkness they move who bow to ignorance; in yet denser darkness they who are satisfied with knowledge.'[1] 'He who recognizes both knowledge and ignorance [as insufficient], he, through both overpasses death and wins immortality.'[2]

The limitations of the either/or position are illustrated by the old question as to whether a river is its banks or the water flowing between them, to which the answer is 'both' since neither would be effective without the other.

The Tao itself partakes of this nature, being both the Way of Heaven and the Way of Earth. Man travels towards the spiritual freedom of enlightenment but along the limited path of conformity to the laws of Nature. A parallel to the Taoist nature-orientated Way is found in the Red Indian outlook which has more than a kinship with the shamanism of pre-Lao Tzu, and again with later popular Taoism. There are striking similarities between the traditions of the Red Indian and Taoism and Hinduism, notably in their cosmology. The Great Spirit of the Red Indian and the basis of natural and cosmological lore in their religion, far from being pantheistic, is much nearer the impersonal Tao and the Natural of Taoism and the Atman of Hinduism as a great, impersonal power beyond expression. Various authorities on mysticism have made clear the difference between it and pantheism. Dean Inge said that 'in mysticism God is really everything, while in ordinary pantheism everything is God'.[3] This is also expressed by Professor Oman as: 'To the Pantheist God is wholly immanent, all is God. To mysticism God is all.' And Santayana makes the point that 'Pantheism, even when psychic, ignores ideals'. It also lacks the transcendent element. In mysticism there is no loss in an amorphous collectivity. 'He who sees Me everywhere and sees everything in Me, I am not lost to him nor is he lost to Me.'[4]

It is the loss of nature-orientation inevitable in the concrete jungle of cities which J. Epes Brown deplores when he says that the Indians are being destroyed 'by a civilization which is out of balance precisely because it has lost those values by which the American Indian lived'.

The Great Spirit is a transcendent Unity, and in that Unity, manifest in the created world, all natural forms are sacred. Animals, being created before man, are nearer to the Great Spirit and not being self-conscious, are more natural and in direct rapport with Nature and the Great Spirit and so should be respected. Black Elk says: 'We regard all created beings as sacred and important, for everything has *wochangi* or influence, which can be given to us, through which we may gain a little more understanding if we are attentive. We should understand well that all things are works of the Great Spirit. We should know that He is within all things; the trees and grasses, the rivers and mountains and all four-legged animals and the winged peoples; and even more important we should understand that He is also above all these things and people.'

In this simple and profound testimony we have the perfect expression of the transcendent and immanent, free from any pantheism since it does not 'equate God with his manifest forms'. 'Peace ... comes within the souls of men when they realize their oneness with the universe and all its powers, and when they realize that at the centre of the universe dwells the Great Spirit and that this centre is really everywhere, it is within each of us.' Black Elk also gives an account of the mystic experience: 'I saw more than I can tell and I understood more than I saw, for I was seeing in a sacred manner the shapes of all things in the Spirit and the shape of all shapes as they must live together like one being ... That is the real world that is behind this one, and everything we see here is something like a shadow from that world. I knew that the real was yonder and the darkened dream of it was here.'

Mysticism speaks a universal language and appears in many philosophies and most religions, a notable exception being

Zoroastrianism. Far from being a dreamy and impractical state of mind it is 'the habit of mind which discerns the spiritual in common things'.[5] 'It repudiates intellectualism, not intellect, moralism, not morality.' In fact, Taoism, which in its classical form, is the most intellectual of religions is also pure mysticism. It is the way of direct apprehension and is a clear-cut path to Enlightenment, to the 'flight of the Alone to the Alone'. It is not a 'branch' of any religion but the ultimate goal. The mystic experience is the realization of cosmic harmony, the expansion of the self until it embraces and merges with the whole and at the same time contains the whole.

9

THE ONE IN
WORLD SCRIPTURES

This Wholeness, or Oneness, with the Tao, The Absolute, the Divine Ground, called by various names, is in no way confined to Taoism. It appears universally, in all traditions, in their scriptures and the teachings of their sages and saints. As the early Buddhist sage, Saraha, puts it: 'There is one Lord revealed in many Scriptures'.

All Scriptures are presented on two levels, the exoteric and the esoteric. On the exoteric level, for the general, unitiated public, there are the creation stories, narratives which deal with the birth of consciousness, of the phenomenal world and the elements. The esoteric level is for the initiated and those who have 'ears to hear' and who can 'see' beyond the realm of the senses; it teaches that the world of multiplicity and objectivity is a reflected world, deceptive or illusory, but which, nevertheless, can, and should be, a means of revealing the Reality it reflects. It can be penetrated by immediate experience. Real knowledge, truth, is only gained through this direct experience; all else is merely knowledge 'about' something. 'Evidence of truth can only lie in man's experience of it.' The esoteric aspects of world scriptures and their metaphysical teachings thus refuse, or ignore, any attempt at proof. Proof belongs to the realm of facts and the senses, not to the realm of ideas which reflect the higher levels. There is no question here of a chosen élite. The teachings are open to anyone who is prepared to take the necessary journey, 'path', or 'way', first to self-knowledge, then to knowledge of the Self, the all-embracing Tao. On the exoteric level many of the historic religions and their sects are exclusive and only those within their narrow beliefs are 'saved'. On the metaphysical and esoteric level there is no such exclusion, the only exclusive factor is the ignorance of the individual and it is open to him or her to abandon this and learn at any time.

It matters in life whether one adopts a materialistic-humanist or a metaphysical point of view since it makes a difference to one's whole response to living. The humanist-materialist deals with quantitative knowledge, immense in its scope, but external and largely useless and often dangerous; inner and qualitative knowledge is either ignored or actively repudiated. Metaphysics assumes an inner meaning, an intellect beyond the human brain and powers above the human level, and beyond them the Absolute, the Tao, which depends on no-thing, but on which all things depend. Tolstoy said: 'We must remind ourselves as often as possible that our true life is not this external, material life that passes before our eyes here on earth, but that it is the inner life of our spirit, for which the visible life serves as a scaffolding – a necessary aid to our spiritual growth. The scaffolding itself is only of temporary importance, and, after it has served its purpose, is no longer wanted but even becomes a hindrance.' It is 'a boundary limiting the free development of our spirit. Matter is the limit of spirit. But true life is the destruction of this limitation. In this understanding of life lies the very essence of the under-standing of truth ... materialists mistake that which limits life for life itself.'

The higher levels of existence must be first recognized then realized. This is true of even such apparently materially concerned disciplines as science where, to quote Bacon: 'No perfect discovery can be made upon a flat or level; neither is it possible to discover the more remote and deeper parts of any science and ascend not to a higher science'. This is echoed in modern times by the physicist Max Planck who writes: 'I have said that the first step which every specialized branch of science takes consist of a jump into the region of metaphysics ... there are fundamentals that cannot be defined or explained ... every definition must necessarily rest on some concept which does not call for definition at all'.

Mankind appears to be equipped by nature for worship and to recognize the existence of powers greater than itself and to feel the need for self-knowledge leading to the knowledge of those powers. If this instinct is denied, abandoned or derided other gods are set up to worship instead – Progress, Science, Evolution and the Superman, these become the holy, the authoritative and unchallengeable. But it can happen that some deep experience or shock can project one into a state of mind beyond what is regarded as the normal. As Browning says:

> Just when we are safest, there's a sunset touch,
> A fancy from a flower-bell, someone's death,
> A chorus-ending from Euripides –
> And that's enough for fifty hopes and fears
> As old and new at once as nature's self,
> To rap and knock and enter in our soul.

Every great religion asserts that man can make no greater mistake than imagining that he is no more than a body and mind. This is the great illusion, the very essence of *maya*. It fails to see that there is a reality behind the appearance of this world, a spiritual or heavenly archetype, the essence, the Ideal Form of Plato. In the words of Hermes: 'All the shapes and images which you see with your bodily eyes in the world of things that come to be and cease to be are mere semblances and copies of the forms which have real existence in the thought-world, those forms which are eternal and will never cease to be'.

Materialism and humanism recognize only the body and its senses, a small part, and at that the least important, of the individual's whole being and potentialities, which should, indeed, be taken as only the first stage of learning and knowledge; they should be accepted and perfected as the instrument of further and higher knowledge and awareness. In themselves mortal and evanescent, understanding through them can only be limited. To quote the Parsee sage Azar Kaivan: 'The knowledge of evanescent objects is not properly knowledge, but bears the same relation to reality as the mirage of the desert to water, the searcher after which obtains nothing but an increase of thirst'.

Materialism is based on quantitative knowledge, entirely outward-looking, sometimes interesting but, again, often dangerous when it is not controlled by the qualitative, inward, supra-human knowledge which is the basis of metaphysics and the teachings of all scriptures which assume that man is more than the aggregate of the body and its senses, and that the way to find this 'more' quality is first to know oneself and then to set out on the path, or way, to enlightenment. For René Guénon metaphysics is 'to know what is, and to know it in such a fashion as to be oneself, truly and effectively, what one knows'. This, of course, is equally the definition of the Taoist sage who is a living embodiment of his knowledge and understanding.

The conceit of the humanist-materialist is remarkable and monumental in supposing man, with a finite brain, to have all the answers. Chuang Tzu and Socrates both laugh at this attitude; Chuang Tzu asserting of such a person – 'You blaze along as though the sun and moon were under your arms', while Socrates asks: 'Do you believe that you have any wisdom within you ... and do you still suppose that there is no spark of wisdom anywhere else in the world ... and do you still think that mind alone is nowhere else to be found and that you have somehow gathered it up as if you had come upon it by some happy accident?' This presumptuous attitude is extended also to Nature. The materialist thinks of himself as conquering Nature and assumes that her laws are merely mechanical. He is the child of the Cartesian aberration which speaks of mankind as 'masters and possessors of Nature', instead of part of it. If results are anything to go by, his efforts at mastery so far appear anything but felicitous, destroying faster than he can create and destroying that which he does not know how to re-create. He has let the djinn out of the bottle and now it towers above him, huge, menacing, terrifying, threatening him with a power he has released but cannot control.

Taoism may be said to agree with humanism in pro-pounding the doctrine of the natural goodness of man and his potentiality for perfection, but it parts company sharply when it comes to the humanist's worship of the god Reason, who will do for man in the future all that he has failed to do in the past. For Taoism, reason is but one faculty among many and one that is as capable of misleading as of leading. It misleads man into strange superstitions, such as believing in his own infallibility and finally into the ultimate error, that he is God himself, able to control destiny, his own and that of all creatures with which he comes in contact.

When Chinese philosophers of both Taoist and Confucian schools spoke of 'human nature' they did not refer to the merely physical nature but to man made in the divine or 'Heavenly' image, which implied the spirituality and perfection proper to man. 'What is Heaven-born is what we call human nature.' He is human when he conforms to that standard, but sub-human when he falls below it. As has been said, he occupies the central position, that of mediator, between Heaven and Earth. 'The highest form of man is he who adapts to and keeps pace with the movement of Tao.'

For the non-materialist, the religionist, metaphysician, the mystic, there is an ultimate reality beyond the body and mind. There is an inalienable belief in a meaning in life which is common to philosophers, religionists, scientists and ordinary man. Originally philosophy, religion and science worked together and maintained a careful control on knowledge, keeping esoteric and in the hands of those capable of wise judgement and administration any knowledge which would be dangerous in the possession of the undisciplined or unwise. With the separation of these branches of knowledge came the materialistic-deterministic outlook and man began to feel himself lost in an alien environment, torn between his instinctive sense of a meaning in life and a mechanistic meaninglessness. Now the philosopher is no longer expected to live his philosophy, his life may be chaotic, divorced from what he teaches, and religion and science have broken away into separate disciplines.

Metaphysics, ('meta', 'after' or 'beyond', physics) is an old term. Aristotle called it 'the first philosophy' or theology. It assumes that man can attain to knowledge which truly and effectively enables him to advance to higher states above the merely psycho-physical, knowledge which, in so raising him, brings about a condition in which he must live his beliefs, as does the sage. For metaphysics, the measure of life is that which is beyond the physical and a knowledge which is beyond the thinking mind. This knowledge is achieved through a total awareness, from which rises spontaneity, a principle central to Taoism, Hinduism and Buddhism. 'Buddha', or wisdom, is used in a sense of 'felt knowledge' in which the subject as such knows itself as subject in the process of being aware. Spontaneity brings freedom; there is no freedom while everything is conceptualized. Only in freedom can Unity, the ultimate goal of the mystic, be reached, in which, as Eckhart says, 'the known and the knower are one'. This is called by Shao Yung, a Taoist of the Sung dynasty, 'the Supreme Limit' – 'The primordial being, from which came all that exists is Tao, the Supreme Limit, the August Limit; but these are only borrowed names; for this primordial being is indefinable, un-namable and ineffable. Heaven and Earth are not of a different nature from the rest of creation; they are the two intermediaries (the *yin* and the *yang*) whereby the Supreme Limit produces everything else ... Beginnings and endings, births and deaths, are simply transformations of those two entities. All things are One.'

Things are only separate existentially and rationally, not essentially. The ultimate unity is not merely that of the individual attaining realization, but that which embraces the whole universe. It has been expressed as the waters of the ocean which are one; only the troughs and waves appearing to differ individually. It is a process of merging and assimilation which results in final identity and inseparability. Here one might quote Sri Ramakrishna: 'It is one and the same Avatara that, having plunged into the ocean of life, rises up in one place and is known as Krishna, and diving down again rises up in another place and is known as Christ. The Avataras stand in relation to the Absolute Brahma as the waves of the ocean are to the ocean.'

In the monotheistic religions, the mystic union is generally expressed in terms of lover and beloved, but they clearly place the relationship outside the individual. The non-theistic religions seldom use this symbolism; union is an inner realization, which can be gradual or immediate, of the Oneness of all things in Brahma, the Tao or Nirvana. But the scriptures and sages of all religions and all ages ultimately speak with the same voice, for, as the French mystic Louis-

Claude de Saint-Martin said: 'All mystics speak the same language, for they come from the same country', or as a modern French writer describes it; 'The wind, Nature's flute, breathing in the trees and on the waters, sings many melodies. In a like way the Tao, the great doctrine, expresses itself through many different minds and many ages, yet remains always the same.' This echoes the ancient Buddhist teaching in the Avatamsaka Sutra that 'In a single country of the Buddha are included all the countries of the Buddha'.

This essential unity of all teachings in all traditions can be demonstrated best by letting them speak for themselves. In Hinduism, according to the *Rig Veda:*

> Agni is One, only kindled in many places.
> One is the Sun mightily overspreading the world.
> One alone is the Dawn beaming over all this.
> It is the One that has severally become all this.

As the Yoga-Vasishtha says: 'Whatever happens, in any form or at any time or place, is but a variation of the One Self-existent Reality'. In modern times Sri Ramakrishna asserted: 'Siva, Kali and Hari are but different forms of that One. He is blessed indeed who has known all as one.' Sri Ramana Maharshi expresses it, 'As the string in (a necklet of) gems, it is Thou in Thy Unity who penetratest all the diversity of beings and religions'.

Taoism, in the *Tao Te Ching*, says that 'The sage keeps to One and becomes the standard for the world', while Chuang Tzu declared: 'I guard the original One, and rest in harmony with externals'. He also maintained: 'The Universe and I came into being together, and I, and everything therein are One', and, 'All things, regardless of their separation and construction, will again bring to the One'.

In Chinese Buddhism the Third Patriarch, Seng-ts'an, said: 'In the Not-Two are no separate things, yet all things are included ... the One is none other than the All, and the All is none other than the One'. And at another time:

One in All,
All in One –
If only this is realized,
No more worry about your not being perfect!

When Taoism and Buddhism met they formed a natural alliance which gave birth to the Ch'an School of Buddhism, later known as Zen in Japan. Chih-k'ai, an early Chinese Buddhist, whose teachings were the foundation of Japanese Buddhism, states that 'Buddhas and all sentient beings are essentially one', and, with Buddhism established in Japan, the later Zen Master Hakuin repeated the same theme: 'All aspects of the universe – the relative and the absolute – are in reality but one'.

In Qabalism, the Ain Aoph is the 'One without a second', and in the *Zohar, The Book of Splendour*, the mystic teaching of Judaism, we read that 'If one contemplates the things in mystical meditation, everything is revealed as one'; and from the same source: 'Lord of the worlds! Thou art One.'

From Christianity, especially in its mystical aspect, endless examples of this realization of unity could be quoted. Early Christianity testifies, in *The Epistle to the Corinthians*, that 'There are diversities of gifts, but the same Spirit. And there are diversities of ministrations, and the same Lord. And there are diversities of workings, but the same God, who worketh all things in all.' This is echoed later by the German mystic Suso, who said: 'All this diversity is fundamentally and basically one single unity', and by Eckhart, who taught: 'All is one and one is all in all', and again with Boehme: 'God is all in all: only one, not many, one in all, and all in one'.

In Islam, the Qur'an states categorically: 'He, Allah, is One – Allah, the Absolute Plenitude'. Unity is particularly stressed in the mystical aspect, Sufism, where, again, the symbolism of the union of Lover and Beloved is frequently employed, but the Sufi metaphysician Jili expresses it in purely metaphysical terms: 'Here the All is both One and Many. Marvel at the plutality of what is essentially One.'

Outside the religions and their scriptures the voices of the sages and philosophers speak in equally unequivocal terms. Xenophanes states laconically: 'All is One', as Hermes says: 'The whole is one', and Plotinus is as simply direct in saying:

'The One is all things and no one of them'. On the other side of
the world the same plain truth is expressed by the Sioux Red
Indian, Black Elk: 'All are really one'. Alchemy also testifies
that 'Nature may truly be described as being *one*, true, simple
and perfect in her own essence'.

So one could go on quoting indefinitely. All is summed up
in Sri Ramakrishna's assertion that 'Hindus, Mussulmans and
Christians are going to the same destination by different
paths', and, as the *Srimad Bhagavetam* says: 'Like a bee
gathering honey from different flowers, the wise man accepts
the essence of different scriptures and sees only the good in all
religions'.

10

KNOWLEDGE

Important as they are, the Scriptures are but a means of leading beyond themselves to direct understanding.

'Listen to this!' shouted Monkey. 'After all the trouble we have had getting here from China, and after you specially ordered that we were given the Scriptures, Ananda and Kasyapa made a fraudulent delivery of goods. They gave us blank copies to take away; I ask you, what is the good of that to us?'

'You needn't shout', said the Buddha, smiling. 'As a matter of fact, it is such blank scrolls as these that are the true Scriptures. But I quite see that the people of China are too foolish and ignorant to believe this, so there is nothing for it but to give them copies with some writing on.'

The same beyond-the-scriptures teaching is also in Shih-T'ou's – 'What is the ultimate teaching of Buddhism? You won't understand it until you have it.'

All traditions assert that the first step towards the attainment of higher levels of understanding, to direct apprehension, the ability to read the blank pages, is the overcoming of the self, or ego, symbolized by Monkey in Wu Ch'eng-en's incomparable masterpiece. It is also to abandon the trivial, the diversifying and dissipating and to awaken to the urgency of the search for the real Self, and this must start with self-knowledge. It is impossible to surpass the self if it is not first understood and controlled. As A.K. Coomaraswamy says: 'The expression "self-control" implies that there is one that controls and another subject to control ... on the one hand body-and-soul (or-mind), and on the other spirit, one is mutable and mortal, the other constant and immortal; one "becomes", the other "is".'

The dictum 'Know Thyself' was made famous in the West through the Delphic inscription to Apollo, but it is far older than that and occurs in all traditions in the world, both in their scriptures and in the teachings of their sages and saints. All religions instruct their followers to look within. This, however, does not imply a morbid self-absorption and introspection, for to know oneself presupposes knowledge of all its relationships and reactions in the outside world also, while self-knowledge is just as important for the understanding of the outer relationships. As has been said, one cannot love one's neighbour as oneself without first knowing and experiencing love in oneself, so it is impossible to understand one's neighbour without first knowing oneself. Nor does self-knowledge mean preoccupation with the psychic faculties; it is a knowledge intended to transcend these and to attain to the spirit. Man studies himself, the microcosm, and its laws, in order to understand the universe, the macrocosm, in which he exists. This demands a much more rigorous discipline than any other form of knowledge-seeking. Self-knowledge is concerned with the quality, not the quantity, of knowledge gained, it is a total awareness, not an analytical dissection, a building up, not a breaking down. It aims at direct knowledge which transcends thought. But Sri Ramana Maharshi points out that 'absence of thought does not mean a blank. There must be one to know the blank. Knowledge and ignorance are of the mind. They are born of duality. But the Self is beyond knowledge and ignorance. It is light itself.' *The Tao Te Ching* says: 'He who knows others is wise. He who knows himself is enlightened', while Chuang Tzu maintains that 'He who knows what Heaven is and who knows what man is, has attained. Knowing what Heaven is, he knows that he himself proceeded therefrom'. Also: 'The sages of old first got Tao for themselves, then got it for others'. The mediaeval writer T'u

Lung expresses it as: 'One who has attained the Tao is master of himself, and the universe is dissolved for him'.

This is the testimony of Taoism, but every tradition echoes the same theme: 'He who has exhausted all his mental constitution knows his nature. Knowing his nature he knows Heaven.' In the Upanishads we read: 'Having realized his own self as the Self, a man becomes selfless', and in the same vein, in modern times, Sri Ramana Maharshi taught: 'See yourself first and then see the whole world as the Self'. Buddhism speaks through the voice of the Zen Master Hakuin: 'When you wake up you will find that this whole world, above and below, is nothing other than a regarding of oneself'. There is also a complete discourse on every branch of self-knowledge in the Buddha's *The Setting-up of Mindfulness*. The Hermetic tradition teaches: 'You ought, O Soul, to get sure knowledge of your own being, and of its forms and aspects. Do not think that any one of the things of which you seek to get knowledge is outside of you; no, all things that you ought to get knowledge of are in your possession, and within you'. Plotinus says the same: 'He who reflects upon himself, reflects upon his own original'.

From earliest times Christianity has put forward the doctrine, first in the words of Christ and later through its scholars, saints and mystics, that 'the Kingdom of Heaven is within you'. Clement of Alexandria asserted that 'If a man knows himself, he shall know God'. This is expressed by Eckhart as: 'I say no man knows God who knows not himself first', while his contemporary Ruysbroeck declared that 'Knowledge of ourselves teaches us whence we come, where we are, and whither we are going'. The Roman philosopher Boethius puts it in a different way when he says that 'In other living creatures ignorance of self is nature; in man it is vice'. For Islam ibn Arabi testifies that 'Man must first of all know his own soul before he can know his Lord; for his knowledge of the Lord is as the fruit of his knowledge of himself', while the Persian Sufi mystic and poet Ansari, in a pithy little poem, writes:

If thou canst walk on water
Thou art no better than a straw.
If thou canst fly in the air
Thou art no better than a fly.
Conquer thy heart
That thou mayst become somebody.

As a method of gaining knowledge, the Eastern religions in general, and the monotheistic religions in their mystic aspects, use the negative way, or *via negativa*, propounded in the Hindu teaching in the Upanishads: 'The significance of Brahman is expressed by *neti, neti* (not this, not that); for beyond this, that you say it is not so, there is nothing further. Its name, however, is the Reality of reality.' It is a process of stripping off layers of unreality and illusion to reach the core of Reality. The 'this' and 'that' belong to duality, to separation, and must be abandoned to attain true knowledge and final unity. In Christianity Eckhart employs the same negative, stripping-away technique in saying: 'Thou must love God as not-God, not-Spirit, not-person, not-image, but as He is, a sheer, pure absolute One, sundered from all two-ness, and in whom we must eternally sink from nothingness to nothingness'. Philo the Jew, steeped in Hellenism, had, long before Eckhart, said: 'He who thinks that God has any quality and is not One, injures not God but himself'. This is expressed by the Christian mystic Nicholas of Cusa as: 'God who is the Maximum is neither this nor that' and says that 'an understanding of God is not so much an approach towards something as towards nothing'. Aquinas says: 'We cannot know what God is, but rather what He is not'. Dante tells us that 'Only by negation can we come to know these things'. In Islam the Sufi Abi l-Khayr said that it had been revealed to him that he was 'neither this nor that'. Huang-po, the Chinese Buddhist, of the Ch'an school, tells us that 'from discrimination between this and that a host of demons blazes forth'.

Dionysius the Areopagite compares the negative way with the work of a sculptor. 'For this is not unlike the art of those who carve a life-like image from stone, removing from around it all that impedes clear vision of the latent form, revealing its hidden beauty solely by taking away.'

This *via negativa* is pre-eminently the Taoist Way, well

expressed by Fung Yu-lan in his *Spirit of Chinese Philosophy:*

> The Taoists' method of seeking the highest kind of knowledge and the highest sphere, was that of discarding knowledge. The fruit of discarding knowledge is no-knowledge, but this kind of no-knowledge comes from having passed through a stage of knowledge. It is not the no-knowledge of original ignorance ... The man with the no-knowledge of ignorance lives in the unselfconsciously natural sphere, the man with the post-gained no-knowledge lives in the transcendent sphere ... The man in the unselfconsciously natural sphere does not know how to make a lot of distinctions between things. The man in the sphere of the transcendent has forgotten the distinctions which he used to make between things ... He is one who, having made distinctions, has forgotten them. The other man who has not made distinctions, has not reached that level.

Of distinctions Chuang Tzu says: 'There is in reality neither truth nor error, neither yes nor no, nor any distinction whatsoever, since all – including the contraries – is One'. He also advised: 'Do not ask if the Principle is this or that', and, again, following Lao Tzu's 'The Tao that can be named is not the eternal Tao; the name that can be defined is not the unchanging name', he says: 'The Principle cannot be heard: that which is heard is not It. The Principle cannot be seen: that which is seen is not It. The Principle cannot be uttered: that which is uttered is not It ... one can neither ask nor reply what It is.' Lao Tzu asserts that the Way is 'subtracting and yet again subtracting'.

The negative way, or the way of self-enquiry, or any other way to self-knowledge is to change oneself so that one is able to see from different aspects and levels; one can only know and understand what one *is*. Knowledge is an integral part of being. Truth remains the same, only the individual adapts to different modes of understanding of it.

11

TAOISM AND HINDUISM

At the ancient capital of China at Ch'ang-an there existed a
wide variety of religious faiths, with worship at their temples
and shrines well established. Taoist and Confucianist temples
represented the indigenous beliefs, while Buddhist shrines,
Zoroastrian fire temples, Nestorian Christian churches
Islamic mosques and Manichaean and Jewish groups continued
peacefully side by side. Most died out as being alien to the
Chinese temperament and mentality, but Buddhism, born of
Hinduism, remained to become the third religion of China
and was largely transformed into a distinctive Chinese Buddhism, and, fusing with Taoism, became Ch'an or Zen.

The comparison of Taoism with other religions is necessarily
superficial in a small space, but it can provide an outline and
indication for further interest. There are basic similarities in
the perennial philosophy of all religions and, of necessity, they
interact with one another, but similarities are not to be
confused with identity; outwardly they are not one, they are
many; it is the Power within them that is One. It is, naturally, in
the mystic aspects of other religions that they have an affinity
with Taoism and that in their dogmatic and theological forms
that they part company.

Hinduism, like Taoism, lays stress on understanding rather

than on action, so that ignorance becomes the opposite of the good and hence is the only real sin. The overcoming of ignorance is *avidya*, and ignorance as the source of all troubles is a common teaching in Hinduism, Taoism and Buddhism. Self-knowledge, *moksha*, is the road to emancipation and the realization of the state of liberation from the illusions of the sense world. The doctrine of the *maya*, or illusion, does not imply that this world is totally unreal but that it is a shadow-play, a reflection. It is the world of space and time, of extension and duration, of relativity, and is only real within its own boundaries; so also is evil in the world limited. *Maya*, although the doctrine does not appear specifically in Taoism, is reflected in manifestation in the in-breathing and out-breathing, creation and return, the evolution and involution of the *yin-yang*. It is only in the world of *maya* that duality exists, subject and object in Hinduism and Taoism are not ultimate entities but are involved in the play of forces in opposition which are to be overcome in the search for enlightenment and the final union of the self with the Self.

There is something reminiscent of the Taoist Hermit in the Hindu Forest Dweller: 'I will take my lodging at the root of a tree, surrendering all things, loved as well as unloved, tasting neither grief nor pleasure, neither cherishing hope nor offering respect, free from the opposites, with neither fortune nor belongings'. This, however, seems to lack the joy in nature characteristic of the Taoist attitude, although, on the other hand, for Hinduism the world is essentially an expression of delight, the play, *lila*, of the Absolute, which, however, is in no way bound by its creation.

Maya is basically the illusion which divides reactions and relationships into subject and object and gives rise to the pairs of opposites in the manifest world, seeing them as separate instead of totally interdependent. The word 'illusion' is derived from the Latin to play a game, but play has its own rules, it is not haphazard, there are winning or losing choices and moves and throws which influence the outcome of the game and set an irrevocable force in motion. *Maya* is also that which can be measured and therefore involves limitation and finitude as opposed to the immeasurable and unbounded Absolute, Atman or Tao. Yet another aspect of *maya* is that of a veil which can both conceal and reveal. It is illusory simply because it is a partial view and partial truth: only the whole truth is illuminating. The viewpoint alters with the level of perception and awareness, as, for example in the classic case of the snake and the coil of rope; the amount of light available for seeing and the ability to observe accurately can completely change the thing seen. Any viewing from outside is liable to distortion. The lower levels are certainly contained in the higher, but it is only from the higher level that it can be appreciated that the other levels are lower, partial truths. They still partake of the nature of truth, but only in a fragmentary manner. The level of manifestation is a limitation in the realm of becoming which is ultimately transcended to reach the level of Being and Truth.

Maya is a reflected world. It is illusory in that the reflection can never be the Thing-in-itself, but it is real in that the reflections can shadow forth the presence of the Real and, once known for what it is, can be the means of leading to the Real. In this reflected world things merely appear distinct and discrete because they are caught up in the time-space continuum and seem to follow each other; the coming into being and passing from it are illusions of time. This succession of changes is perceived by mind and created by mind. 'All difference is due to time, space and causation. These are the constituent element of mind. No mentality is possible without them. You can never think without time, you can never imagine anything without space, you can never have anything without causation. These are the forms of mind. Take them away and the mind itself does not exist. All difference is therefore due to the mind ... qualities are born of the mind. That which is qualityless must be one ... everything in the universe is that One, appearing in various forms.'[1]

One branch of Indian idealism speaks of 'perfuming', just as the clothes we wear have no personal scent of their own but take on a distinctive aroma when worn. The real 'suchness' or 'that which is' is the original thing-in-itself which is untainted by 'perfuming', which comes from ignorance and is the power of illusion in the world. 'That which is' is pure, that which is manifest is tainted by duality and becomes an illusion of the ego and of separateness. Once the ignorance and illusion are recognized the 'perfuming' power works in reverse and leads to an understanding of the truth and releasing from the bonds of illusion, leading the individual to the *dharma* and the way back to the Real.

Awareness, *cit*, is the Essence which makes possible the transcendence of the realm of illusion of the senses in the phenomenal world. The system of Patanjali aims more at the control of the mind than at union with the ultimate and appears to accept a fundamental dualism not present in Taoism. The dualism of *purusa* and *prakriti*, subject and object is absolute in Samkhya, the yoga of Patanjali, each having its own eternal existence, as opposed to the non-dualistic school of *Vedanta* which is committed to belief in the Absolute, a Supreme Being with which union is possible. The God of *Advaita-Vedanta* is the efficient cause of the Universe; from Brahman issues the whole cosmos: in manifestation 'It' is Isvara, or any other divine name.

Hinduism is rightly and naturally polytheistic in the world of manifestation, but monotheistic in the doctrine of the One, Brahman. Apparent polytheism is, in fact, a unified plurality, or the action in multiplicity of the One. A pantheon also appeared in late Taoism, borrowed largely from Buddhism which had carried over much from Hinduism.

In the Upanishads, Brahman and Atman are names expressing the Primordial Principle, or Tao; they do not imply a deity to be worshipped in any personal sense, but express that which is beyond all forms and phenomena but from which all has arisen. In It all dualities are resolved. It may be fully equated with the Tao as impersonal Spirit, the Supreme Power of the universe, beyond the reach of the senses and the rational mind; It is the unqualified and limitless. 'Brahman has neither name nor form, transcends merit and demerit, it is beyond time, space and the objects of sense-experience. Such is Brahman, and thou art That'. 'Supreme, beyond the power of speech to express, Brahman may yet be apprehended by the eye of pure illumination. Pure, absolute and eternal Reality.' Of Atman it is said: 'Grasping without hands, hastening without feet, it sees without eyes, it hears without ears. It knows what is to be known, but no one knows it.'[2] 'From it the universe comes forth, into it the universe merges and in it the universe breathes.'[3] Taoism parallels this with: 'When the Ten Thousand Things are viewed in their oneness, we return to the Origin and remain where we have always been.'[4] And there is no better definition of the Tao than Krishna's saying: 'I, oh Arjuna, am that which is and that which is not'.[5]

What for Sri Ramana Maharshi is the Self, is in every respect applicable to the Tao. The Self cannot be 'attained' since, like the Tao, it is all and contains all; it must be realized, but even then that expression involves the implication of separation. It is rather a case of 'be what thou art' or in the Maharshi's own words: 'If the Self were to be reached it would mean that the Self is not now and here, but that it should be got anew. What can be got afresh can also be lost. So it will be impermanent. What is not permanent is not worth striving for. So I say the Self is not reached. You are the Self. You are already That.' Although Taoism does not actually speak of the inner Self as the Tao, it may be fair to say that since 'beyond the Self there is nothing',[6] it may be equated with the Tao.

The Upanishads speak of One Being which divided itself into Two, the male and female, and brought about the existence of the cosmos. Radha and Krishna appear as *shakti* and *shakta*, each deriving power from the interplay and interaction with the other. (Indian symbolism is here expressed in more physical terms that those used in the more abstract Chinese mode.) This is also the symbolism of Shiva and his *shakti* in the upward and downward pointing triangles, representing fire and the male, with water and the female element. These have their counterparts in *purusha*, mind, male, and *prakriti*, matter, female, Essence and Substance. Every Indian deity is balanced by his consort and this *yin-yang* symbolism is evidenced in Hinduism in the representation of the androgynous Siva and Parvati, which involves the full significance of the opposites and complementaries, but is expressed in a more sexual form than the *yin-yang*. Balance is also stressed in the Hindu theory of the qualities of Nature, the two opposites of the active and the inert, the *rajas* and *tamas*, with *sattva*, balance, as the resolving third. A passage from the *Bhagavad Gita*[7] also echoes the Taoist actionless-action of *wu-wei:* 'The action that is obligatory is done without love or hate by one who desires no fruit and who is free from attachment – that action is characterized by *sattva*, balance.'

The *Gita* teaches that it is not necessary to renounce the world. There should be no real conflict between ordinary and spiritual life; all that is necessary is to act without attachment.

'Not by abstention from action does a man enjoy actionless-ness.'[8] This detachment in both Hinduism and Buddhism is the same as the acceptance of Taoism since in each case there is no rejection of the occurrences of daily life, coupled with an acceptance of all experience with an evenness and openness of mind. As Krishna says to Arjuna: 'Neither let your motive be the fruit of action, nor let your attachment be to non-action ... perform your actions casting off attachment and remaining even-minded in success and failure.' 'He who sees inaction in action and action in inaction – he is wise among men, he is a yogi, he has performed all action.'

The yogi, whose aim is union with the Real, the Absolute of non-dualistic Vedanta, recognizes the importance of the body as an instrument for the development of the spiritual and so works for a perfect physical and mental balance which will lead to supra-physical and supra-mental states of awareness. As a preliminary to this realization he must resolve the dualistic conflicts so that he is no longer caught up in the unrealities of *maya*. Rhythm in the physical and mental functions is, as in later Taoism, obtained by breathing and other exercises. Some branches of yoga tended towards asceticism, austerities and world-renunciation, and in Taoism this alien factor crept in with the 'Hygiene School', which attempted to develop the ability to do without food through breathing techniques – literally living on air! This was a radical departure from classical Taoism and yoga, with its 'letting-go' of *wu-wei*, and the natural release from all that is restricting and artificial. There is a vast difference between the controlled practices of yoga in reducing the demands of the sensual and instinctive life and so rendering the body a fit vehicle for the journey towards enlightenment, and the masochistic self-torturing of the body as practised in fakirism and Christian asceticism, which renders the body weak and useless. The yoga of later, decadent Taoism had lost the earlier spiritual aims embodied in Hindu yoga and was directed towards the pursuit of personal immortality through transmutation of the gross body into a subtle body capable of surviving apparent death. The real aim of yoga was ignored or lost, that of union with the One, or the Tao, of metaphysical Taoism. Alchemical Taoism, with its cult of the immortality of the body, had certain affinities with Hatha yoga in this bodily cult and in its name which is solar-luna and so approximates the *yin-yang* or *Shiva-shakti* polarity. There seems to be some confusion as to what was meant by this immortality. In some cases it was undoubtedly a striving for perfect physical health and attempting to find the means of bodily immortality; in other ways it appears more in the nature of an alchemical transformation which, through yoga, formed a higher, non-material, immortal body.

Original Taoism had nothing in common with *bhakti-yoga*, the way of devotion to a personal God, coupled with sacrifice, except in its final aim of union. The intellectual *jnana-yoga* and the contemplative *raja-yoga* were more in accord with traditional Taoism, but *jnana-yoga*, though the way of knowledge and intuition, discrimination and discernment, parts company with Taoism when it teaches renunciation and austerity; not that its austerities were the masochism of the ascetic. *Karma-yoga* has an affinity with the actionless-action of Taoism. Action is an essential part of life, but this action is unattached, unmotivated: 'Therefore, without attachment perform always the work that has to be done, for man attains to the highest by doing work without attachment'.[9]

The *Yogasikha Upanishad* teaches that neither yoga nor knowledge by themselves lead to emancipation, but both should be practised. But meditation and yogic exercises practised merely for the relief of the tremendous tensions of modern life but divorced from their spiritual background, are ultimately more dangerous than helpful since they give temporary relief which imparts a false sense of security but fail to deal with the root of the trouble, spiritual malaise, merely enabling people to live with their illusions instead of curing them.

12

TAOISM AND BUDDHISM

Buddhist priests were said to have arrived in China, from India, at the Chinese capital in the reign of Ch'in Shih-huang-ti, between 221 and 208 B.C. It was said that there were Buddhist monks at Ch'ang-an in the second half of the second century B.C., but these assertions cannot be verified definitely. Traders travelled along the Silk Route and entered North West China at Tun-huang and both they and the Buddhist monks settled in the towns. Later, Chu shih-hsing journeyed to Khotan, in the middle of the third century B.C. to obtain Buddhist scriptures and brought back the Sanscrit *Prajna-paramita*, which greatly influenced Chinese Buddhist thought, while Fa Hu (c. 266-308) translated the Mahayanist *Lotus of the True Doctrine* and in A.D. 399 Fa-hsien left Ch'ang-an on a pilgrimage to India to study sacred texts and to persuade Indian Buddhist teachers to go to China.

The T'ang dynasty saw an increase of pilgrims to India. Hsuan-tsang (c. 596-664) left China in 629 and did not arrive back until 645, having studied at Nalanda University. He brought back sutras and relics in quantity and thereafter did an enormous amount of translation work. In 677 I-sing took the sea route to India from Canton and he both translated and wrote Buddhist works. From Nalanda, Padmasambhava travelled to convert Tibet to Buddhism in the eighth century, developing the distinctive form of Tibetan Buddhism.

Both Sanscrit and classical Chinese were languages of a literary élite and were not available to anyone other than the scholar, so that original Buddhism in China was an intellectual philosophy and found itself closely akin to metaphysical Taoism but had little in common with classical Confucianism, which was based on ethics and regarded the family as a sacred institution and filial piety as a sacred duty; indeed Buddhism actually conflicted with the Confucian ideal in discouraging family life and encouraging celebacy. Also the rigidity of the rules controlling the life of the Confucian scholar was unacceptable to Taoism and Buddhism, both of which laid stress on fluidity and adaptability.

In propagating their religion the early Buddhist missionaries, and their Chinese converts, made considerable use of Taoist philosophy and phraseology in translating the Sutras and in demonstrating the compatibility of the Buddhist faith with the indigenous Taoist culture. For example, in early Buddhism *wu-wei* was used to express Nirvana, as actionless-action, the cessation of dualistic activity; also the Way of Tao was equated with the Path leading to Nirvana, and Buddha was described as 'the one who does nothing yet there is nothing he does not do'. As early Buddhism borrowed from Taoism, so later decadent Taoism borrowed from the pantheon which developed in Buddhism until the two became almost indistinguishable and both popular Taoism and Buddhism shared and were dominated by the ubiquitous spirits, good and bad, which had constantly to be consulted and propitiated.

Buddhism and Taoism are in accord nearly all the way, only diverging in a small, though vital, point: that of the attitude to life's vicissitudes. Buddhism has been accused of pessimism, not altogether fairly, but it does adopt an attitude to life in this world which sees it as suffering, as the result of desire, and as something from which to escape. Taoism, on the other hand, teaches the acceptance of things as they are and views life as something basically good and to be enjoyed, having here an affinity with the Parsee belief in 'the good life'. Taoism also has a more humorous approach to life. Chuang Tzu's book abounds in humour, sometimes mocking and mordant, but laughter is never far off. However, in Buddhism we have

Buddhaghosa speaking of the cheerfulness of the *arhant*, or Sage, 'who is distinguished by and noted for his cheerful temperament',[1] and the Ch'an Master Tao-shin said: 'It is all joy, free from anxiety – it is called Buddha'. The Buddhist teaching on suffering does not imply that all life is misery, but that sorrow and suffering are inevitable in human existence and its aim is to free mankind from that state by going beyond it to enlightenment; the chief means of so doing being to dispel ignorance and see things as they are. Nor does Buddhism encourage the self-inflicted suffering of asceticism: 'By suffering, the emaciated devotee produces confusion and sickly thoughts in his mind. Mortification is not conducive even to worldly knowledge, how much less to a triumph over the senses'.[2] Both Taoism and Buddhism insist on a total living in the present moment, not clinging to or regretting a dead past, nor meeting or speculating on a future before it arrives, but seeing into the present nature of things. There is an Indian saying that you cannot ride the camel that has gone, nor mount the camel that is not yet here. Moment-to-moment living solves problems as they arise, gives a clearer, more direct view of their content and prevents anxiety and worry which always involve a merely hypothetical future which may never come.

Both religions are non-theistic, maintaining that 'God', or the Tao, or Nirvana are beyond conceptual thought; they discourage speculation and 'discursive thought'. Buddha said: 'By allaying the initial and discursive thought, with the mind inwardly tranquillized and fixed on one point, I entered into and abided in the second *jnana* which is devoid of initial and discursive thought ... I dwelt with even-mindedness, mindful and clearly conscious'.

Reason with its clear-cut either/or, right or wrong, fact or fiction, is limited to the manifest world and cannot go beyond it; it has its uses in the realm of duality, but exceeds its legitimate function when it tries to concern itself with the infinite or the ultimate, also, being in duality it must always give rise to conflict and argument and so often it depends on facts which are selected to fit the theories: 'the jungle of theorizing, the wilderness of theorizing, the tangle of theorizing, the bondage and shackles of theorizing, attended by ill, distress, perturbation and fever; it conduces not to detachment, passionlessness, tranquility, peace, to knowledge and wisdom of Nirvana'.[3] Nirvana and the Tao are both the ultimate resolution of all opposites where there is 'neither this world nor any other world, neither sun nor moon',[4] yet 'the life of the world is the same as Nirvana and really there is no difference between them at all'.[5] 'Only those whose minds no longer measure things understand Nirvana which they grasp not nor reject ... for them the three times and both extremes have disappeared.'[6] The Ch'an Master answering the question 'What is Tao?', replied: 'Ordinary life is the very Tao; and 'What is Tao?', – 'Eat when you are hungry and sleep when you are tired'.

Taoism and Ch'an, later Zen in Japan, use the same language; the Self-Nature of Buddhism and the Tao are one and the same. The Sixth Patriarch was told that Ch'an Masters at the capital were teaching that 'if one wishes to understand Tao one should sit in *dhyana* meditation and practise *samadhi*, but the Patriarch replied: 'Tao is to be understood by the awakening mind and has nothing to do with sitting in meditation ... the Tathagata has neither whence to come nor whither to go, because it is beyond birth and death'.[7]

Ch'an was the synthesis of Taoism and Buddhism. The Buddhist Patriarch Bodhidharma, the 'Bearded Barbarian', as the Chinese called him, arrived in China from India at the golden age of Chinese culture. In meeting Taoism the two philosophies had so much in common that it was not surprising that a fusion took place and produced the Ch'an school. It, as with original Taoism and Buddhism, arose as a protest against the development of formalism and speculation and advocated a return to simplicity. Both recognized two methods of attaining enlightenment, gradual progression, or sudden illumination. The sudden or 'abrupt' way aims at shocking the disciple into an immediacy of experience, as Gai Eaton puts it: 'To cut, with a well-aimed thrust, through the curtain which shuts out the light'. Here, the rational mind is a hindrance and source of delusions and limitations; it functions in the realm of the senses, indeed, in Eastern religions it *is* the sixth sense. We are not simple-minded enough and allow both mind and emotions to interfere with direct perception; this is the Taoist-Buddhist doctrine of No-mind.

Taoist and Ch'an masters are indistinguishable and are

represented as wizened men laughing in the face of self-righteousness and worldly values of such things as fame and fortune, taking neither themselves nor anyone else too seriously. Theirs is the effortless-effort, actionless-action, coupled with an inherent lightness of touch and lightness of spirit. Weight is of the earth, lightness is a quality of the spirit. Though remaining impersonal and detached, the personal and immediate are enjoyed in the everyday world in a total freedom from attachment.

Possibly the most significant concept passed on by Taoism into Ch'an is that of immediacy and spontaneity necessary for living in accord with Nature and for simplicity, motiveless action and the perfection of effortlessness. When Ch'an reached Japan and became known as Zen, this spontaneity influenced all branches of Japanese art, in painting, poetry, archery and fencing, all demanding instantaneous response which gives the thinking mind no time to interfere; no deliberation, no alteration is possible, and, as in Taoism, with simplicity and spontaneity come joy, lightheartedness and the totally carefree spirit; of this freedom Hui Neng, the Ch'an Patriarch said: 'The only difference between a Buddha and an ordinary man is that one realizes it and the other does not'. This freedom is also the Taoist *wu-wei*, letting-go, non-assertion, moving with the currents of life and Nature and so avoiding friction and allowing the upsurge of the natural rhythms of life, both physical and spiritual. 'Use the light within you to revert to your natural clearness of sight. No need to look for it outside.'[8]

Hinayana Buddhism has less affinity with Taoism than has the Mahayana; the former, with its stress on the control of the body and its strong dualism, has more in common with later, popular Taoism which developed its own forms of yogic practices, as in alchemical Taoism and the 'hygiene school' which taught breath control, fasting, hygiene and cultivation of the body, as did Hatha yoga; its devotees were vegetarian, abstained from wine and were celebate, their aim being first longevity in a healthy physical and mental state in this life, then a happy survival in the Western Paradise. Earlier Taoism and Mahayana aimed at the development of wisdom in the making of the Sage or Enlightened One and the attaining of the Tao or Nirvana. The Pure Land Buddhism and later Taoism both promulgated the idea of the Western Paradise, to which souls of the virtuous and fortunate gained entrance at death, and early Chinese Buddhism is shown as teaching the existence of an immortal soul; Yüan Hung, of the Han dynasty, wrote in his *Hou Han Chi*, that Buddhists 'also teach that when a man dies his soul does not perish but will be reborn and take another form'. And Hui-yüan wrote: 'While the body dissolves, the spirit does not change. With the unchanging spirit availing itself of the changing body, there is no end to the transformations.'[9] But these teachings were a departure from the original precepts of their founders, since the concept of the Western Paradise conflicted with the non-personal nature of the Tao and the Buddhist Nirvana. Both the Buddhist *Sunyata* and the Taoist Void, Emptiness or Ultimate Reality, are inner, not outward, states and beyond definition. Of *Sunyata* it is written: 'Nothing comes into existence, nor does anything disappear. Nothing is eternal, nor does it have an end.' Of the Tao it is said, 'It is the formless yet complete', it 'stands alone and never changes, it pervades everywhere and is never exhausted'.[10]

Tantric Buddhism, which became specifically the form of Buddhism in Tibet, rose from yogic practices but transcended them. It is an interpretation of a relative dualism such as exists in Hinduism in the symbolism of the *shakti-shakta*, or *Shiva-shakti*, and the union of male and female which appears in a more humanised version of the more abstract *yin-yang* symbol, the union of the two resulting in the merging of their dual identities into the androgyne, the non-dualistic One. This Tantric union is analogous with the marriage of Wisdom and Method, *prajna* and *upaya*, *yin* and *yang*, though Tantric Buddhism does not fully equate the feminine principle with *shakti* so much as with *prajna*, Wisdom, and although employing the female-male polarity, it, like Taoism in the *yin-yang*, implies no sexuality in the symbolism. The one is transcendent and aloof, the other immanent and playing a part in the world. The *yin-yang* symbolism also appears in the concept of the body being composed of two elements, the diamond element, the male, active, material, and the womb element, the female, passive and mental.

S. B. Dasgupta writes of Tantra as: 'a theological principle of duality in non-duality ... The ultimate non-dual Reality possesses two aspects in its fundamental nature, the negative *(nivritti)* and the positive *(pravritti)*, the static and dynamic ... these two aspects are represented in Hinduism by Shiva and Shakti and in Buddhism by *prajna* and *upaya*, or *Sunyata* and *karuna*'.[11]

In Tantrism the senses, which are normally an agent binding man to the body, are used as a means of release from their tyranny and as an aid to the understanding of the relationship of the body to the spirit and the spirit to the divine.

Tantrism and Taoism, however, part company in their practical application for while traditional Taoism was ritual-free, spontaneous and unconventional, Tantrism is highly ritualistic, though one school did maintain that ritual was a hindrance and enlightenment was attained by the sudden stroke or spontaneous illumination.

13

TAOISM AND ZOROASTRIANISM

Although Zoroastrianism, the Good Religion, is a theological and ritualistic, and hence an ethical, tradition, it has points in common with both Taoism and Confucianism. It teaches the dignity and nobility associated with the Mean, the common-sensible, regulated, smooth-running and civilized attitude to life so characteristic of Confucianism and the old Chinese social and personal courtesy. Professor Zaehner's comment on Zoroastrianism that in it 'there is little difference between the ill-bred person and the sinner',[1] would hold equally for the old Chinese code of conduct. Like Confucianism, the religion of Zarathustra also demands absolute justice. Taoism, on the other hand, while not going so far as to suggest actually loving one's enemies, says that one should do good to them, but for all three traditions any attitude of vengeance is an evil and beneath the dignity of the good, the generous and the reasonable man.

Zoroastrianism goes further than either Taoism or Confucianism in its dualistic aspect; instead of the *yin-yang* interplay, each being interdependent and containing the germ of the other within itself and all being in a state of flux, Zoroastrianism offers a sharp division between the opposites of good and evil since 'each exists in and by its own essence in endless antagonism'. 'There never has been anything, nor will there be anything, which is neither good nor evil, nor a mixture of the two.'[2] Everything that exists must belong absolutely to one of these two categories and the one cannot give rise to the other as do the *yin* and the *yang*. Even the animal kingdom is dualistic, either created by and belonging to Ormuzd, such as dogs and birds, or belonging to Ahriman and the powers of evil, such as wolves, cats, snakes and rats. Zoroastrianism parts company with all other Eastern religions which assert that the creative power or principle is a unity; for the Zoroastrian dualism is fundamental in the realm of creation, though it is not eternal as it is in Pythagoreanism, Manichaeism and in the later Christian 'heresies' such as that of the Cathars, since at the end of creation evil will be defeated. But Zoroastrianism comes nearer to Eastern traditions when it equates evil with ignorance, seeing it as a negative quality, or at least a mistake, and at worst a blind, obstinate stupidity. The Good Religion is the mother of wisdom: 'of all things wisdom is the best', and 'right knowledge' is necessary to attain wisdom.

Mankind is regarded as God's finest work in creation, made to combat the forces of evil and bring about their downfall in the defeat of Ahriman; but man also has in himself the contrary qualities of good and evil, so must be ever-watchful and active in fighting for the one and against the other. This duality appears again in the concept of the feminine power which, in its good aspect is Spandarmat, Queen of Heaven and Mother of All Things, and, who like all Queens of Heaven is both the daughter and bride of the Creator, and it is also the Whore, Gayamart, who seduces man and is the evil aspect of the feminine. Having been created by Ormuzd, she must have been good originally, but, allying herself with Ahriman, she seduces man as Eve worked with the Serpent to seduce Adam. So she has both a good and evil aspect, as in all other religions, notably as the Hindu Kali who is both nourisher and destroyer.

The Heaven-Man-Earth relationship, so notable in Chinese tradition, appears in the Zoroastrian creed as 'my Father is Ormuzd', Heaven, the Supreme Light. And 'my Mother is Spandarmat', the Earth. Ormuzd would also appear to be the

'Unmoved Mover' since he created 'without thought, without movement, without touch'. It would seem that in Zoroastrianism there is also the Transcending Third beyond the opposites or alternatives, since Ahura Mazda, Lord of Light and Truth, and Angra Mainu, Lord of Darkness and Lies, were both the children of Zervana Akarana and will ultimately become one with him again.

Zoroastrianism and Taoism meet in the belief in the virtue of naturalness and of co-operation with Nature so that she may grow and produce in accordance with her laws, 'through Nature to Nature's God'. The *Te*, virtue, of Taoism, is to live in accord with Nature, the Way of Tao; the virtue of the Good Life of Zoroastrianism is to derive the best from it and to give the best to it. This 'virtue', as in Taoism, does not preclude or inhibit, but actually encourages, enjoyment of life. Asceticism and extremes are opposed as totally contrary to Nature, to the Good Life and to balance and harmony which it is man's concern to see that he and all dependent on him, animals and plants as well, share in the goodness of the earth. The earth is cared for with a religious devotion and no form of life is exploited. Taoism and Zoroastrianism both actively encourage laughter and a sense of humour, both exhort man to live in the present and to enjoy life, leaving the past and not worrying about the future, but at the same time being conscious of the need for balance and harmony and being neither overjoyed by prosperity nor cast down by misfortune, for the one can turn into the other at any moment. Also, as Chuang Tzu laughed at the infantile desire for fame and fortune, calling them so many fetters, and refusing the office of Prime Minister in favour of freedom, so Zoroastrianism says: 'Do not strain for high office' as this corrupts the spirit.

In the Good Religion, the doctrine of moderation accords with the natural way of Taoism, the Mean of Confucianism, the Middle Way of Buddhism, and the Hellenic 'Nothing Overmuch'. The keynote of balance is evident throughout and all excess and deficiency are deplored and rejected as inconsistent with wisdom and as rendering life ineffective. The Mean keeps the world from the extremes of the realm of the Aggressor. Evil and the Lie, 'the most violent lie', are equated with aggression and violence; to the excess of the Lie is opposed the Mean, the Truth.

Certainly Taoism differs from Zoroastrianism in the precise and somewhat rigid morality of the latter and its cut-and-dry dualism of good and evil, but the two join in saying: 'Do in holiness anything you will', which is the same as the freedom from conventional morality exercised by the Taoist Sage who can do no wrong since it is no longer in him. Again, the Zoroastrian aspect is rather more serious-minded than the light-hearted Taoist attitude.

Taoists share with Zoroastrians the belief that all celestial things have earthly counterparts which are imbued with the spiritual power behind them, so that any art or anything that lacks this spiritual quality and is designed merely to give pleasure is, as Plato says, only a toy, instead of manifesting 'the life movement of the Spirit'.[3]

The namelessness of the Tao – 'The Tao that can be named is not the eternal Tao; the name that can be defined is not the unchanging name'[4] – is echoed in the *Shikand-Gumani Vazar* which says: 'If all things were One, this One would be nameless, for it is only through possession of a name that one thing can be distinguished from another'.

The Void of Zoroastrianism is totally different from that of Taoism. In the former it is that which lies between Light and Darkness, Ormuzd and Ahriman, it is the 'instrument' with which to combat the powers of Darkness and of the Lie in the battle for Light and Truth, and into which evil is finally hurled. This Void, or Vay, becomes a force in itself and is deified. The Void of Taoism is that from which all emanates and to which all returns, the Pleroma, and it is nearer the Zoroastrian Boundless Time which was before the universe was made manifest, without beginning or end, whereas Limited Time, a self-created Time which can be measured, started when the Sun, Moon and stars were created.

Ormuzd, or Ahura Mazda, is Lord of both spirit and matter, the *yang* and the *yin* and both come from the same source. The Supreme Being, like the Tao, is formless and incomprehensible to the finite mind, it is only revealed to man through its aspect of rays from the central Light.

The individual is free to choose between the dualistic powers of Good and Evil, Light and Darkness, Truth and Lies, Life and Life-denial, constructive and destructive forces:

Hear with your ears the highest/Truth I teach,
And with illumined minds weigh them with care,
Before you choose which of two Paths to tread,
Deciding man by man, each one for each.[6]

The emphasis here is on Mind, the 'illuminated mind', which is the decisive power in enabling man to choose, through wisdom, the way of Light and Life. All evil is due to lack of wisdom and intelligence; the sinner is stupid in that he does harm to himself. Once man turns his back on his true self his soul begins to disintegrate and he is no longer human, but before this stage is reached he may suffer for his stupidity and the pain of suffering may lead him to realize his folly and to turn to wisdom. Hinduism, Taoism, Zoroastrianism and Buddhism all lay responsibility for his fate and state of life fairly and squarely on man himself, enjoining self-knowledge and the choice of the right path and offering no vicarious salvation and no mediator for man since he should himself be the mediator between Heaven and Earth, the source and means of balance and harmony.

The basic difference between Taoism and Zoroastrianism is that the latter has no tradition of mysticism, while Taoism is mysticism itself.

A later Persian religion, which followed Zoroastrianism, rose from the teaching of Mani (c. 216-276) and was established as Manichaeism, which flourished for a time then died out in the fourteenth century. It was eclectic, deriving various elements from Zoroastrianism, Buddhism and Christianity, but its main feature was its absolute dualism which had nothing in common with the dualism of the yin-yang since it was absolute and primary; spirit was good, matter evil, which, logically, requires complete rejection of the material world and all that in it is, and therefore condones, if not actually encourages, asceticism. This is totally at variance with Zoroastrian belief which maintains that the world was created good and offers the Good Life to its adherents, and with the Taoist teaching that man is basically good. The contempt for the physical body, evident in later Christianity, was passed down through the Manichaean influence of St Augustine. In China

Manichaeism was established and spread during the T'ang dynasty; the T'ang Emperors received Zoroastrian and Manichaean representatives at court and allowed them to establish temples. Both religions continued there through the Sung and Yüan dynasties until they were absorbed and finally died out. The Manichaean contempt for the body never found an echo in Taoism where the body was first regarded as an instrument of the spirit, to be kept in the *yin-yang* balance, then later given an exaggerated care in the cult of longevity and the search for the elixir of immortality.

14

TAOISM AND THE
MONOTHEISTIC RELIGIONS

Broadly speaking, the religions of the Orient, and particularly the non-theistic Taoism and Buddhism, follow the path of knowledge, gnosis and realization, while the theistic religions, having a personal God, take the path of devotion and sacrifice or the *bhakti* way. Theistic religions must, by definition, assume the existence of a Creator God, a tenet avoided by the non-theistic traditions, which maintain that the Godhead is beyond definition and the range of the human mind, though this attitude, as we shall see, appears also in the sayings of both Christian and Sufi mystics. On the whole, however, the way of devotion and sacrifice leads to a personal love symbolism of the Beloved, always emotional and sometimes bordering on the erotic, employing such terms as 'bride and bridegroom', 'burning love' and the soul 'bringing forth children', an element totally lacking in the intellectual, impersonal mysticism of Taoism and Buddhism. Equally alien to Eastern religions is the idea of vicarious sacrifice; they, as has been said, promulgate the doctrine that man is responsible for his own salvation or degeneration in choosing the path he takes and by regulating his life on moral cause and effect and on the assumption that evil action creates more evil and brings bad *karma* and good deeds create good *karma*, man makes his own destiny, his own heaven or hell. It is of interest to note that this doctrine did appear in Christianity in the Pelagian heresy, which threatened at one time to gain acceptance in Britain; it denied original sin and asserted that free will gave man the choice between right and wrong, the choice bringing its inevitable consequences and setting in train a line of answerable results without any divine influence being at work. This is the nearest that Christianity has come to the doctrine of *karma*, which is explicit in Hinduism and Buddhism and implicit in Taoism.

The monotheistic religions depend essentially on revelation; Moses, Jesus, Mahomet, were the instruments of divine revelation, though this element exists in all religions to a less dominant extent: the Vedas were revealed to the Seers, Buddha revealed wisdom and the Sages of Taoism and Confucianism were also responsible for revealing wisdom to the unenlightened. In one case the revelation is essential and total, in the other it occurs as a result of attaining enlightenment. The monotheistic religions are largely concerned with man's encounter with God, an external viewpoint, while Eastern religions teach that man finds the divine within himself and all things. Generally speaking, it might be said that they way of the monotheistic traditions is that of renunciation and devotion, and that of the non-theistic religions that of knowledge and acceptance. Also pure Taoism and Buddhism, before they developed a pantheon, knew nothing of the capriciousness of gods who 'tempt' or 'test' their devotees, who display human characteristics of anger and jealousy, who cause suffering as well as offering solace, who delight in sacrifice and whose reactions often appear completely unpredictable.

Original Christianity was free from the demanding and rigid morality that went with the 'Thou shalt, or shalt not' attitude, having, in its founder, discarded the retributive position of the Old Testament, and based its teaching on the gentler qualities of love, compassion and understanding of human frailty – accepting the idea of the Kingdom of Heaven within rather than a demanding God without. But while Christ taught that the Kingdom of Heaven was within, Christianity, as it developed, became tied to the concept of striving for a goal of perfection, the progress of 'becoming', a condition arrived at by stages and states. This is contrary to the Taoist-Buddhist teaching of 'being' rather than 'becoming'. Becoming is tied to duality, to a process and a progression, superficial states which must be transcended before time and becoming can stop and being supervene in all its simplicity, spontaneity and fullness. This divergence is largely attributable to the Pauline influence, with its earnest strivings and the repression of the *yin* element and the over-emphasis on the *yang*. Duality was represented as a conflict between the two natures of man, with the consequent guilt complex, instead of the two working in tension, balance and harmony. Christianity owes a great debt to its mystics who not only rectified the Pauline imbalance but helped to free it from slavery to historical fact, when it was too concerned with events in time, and to take it back to the timeless.

The *yin-yang* balance, lost in Paulinism, was restored by the mystics in the two ways of the *via affirmata* and the *via negativa* which require each other, for while the former can affirm qualities of the Deity these are nevertheless attributes and cannot be effective beyond the manifest. Since the Absolute is indefinable and beyond all qualities, so the negative 'not this, not that' must be employed to strip away all that is not in order to reveal that which is.

Balance was also lost in asceticism, such as that practised by Suso and others who tortured themselves and produced the inevitable physical and mental reactions resulting in the Dark Night of the Soul and all the morbid manic-depressive extremes, from which Eckhart, St Teresa of Avila and the English mystics were happily free. Traherne, with mordant logic, says that the ascetics 'put off felicity with long delays and are to be much suspected ... nor can any reason be given why they should desire it at the last and not now'.[1] Joy runs through all Traherne's mysticism: 'A Magnanimous Soul is always awake ... the sun is its lamp, the sea its fishpond, the stars its jewels, men, angels its attendants, and God alone its sovereign delight... the earth is its garden, all palaces its summer houses, cities are its cottages, empires its more spacious Courts, all ages and kingdoms its demeans'.[2] And there is no better expression of the natural in mysticism than his: 'You never enjoy the world aright, till the sea floweth in your veins, till you are clothed with the heavens and crowned with the stars, and perceive yourself to be the sole heir of the whole world, and more than so, because men are in it who are everyone sole heirs as well as you'.

The author of *The Cloud of Unknowing*, a true mystic with a practical turn of mind, humorous and acute, as well as disliking the 'monkey tricks of the soul', deplores the emotionalists who 'travail their fleshly hearts outrageously in their breasts and hurt full sore the silly soul'. Nor does he like pompous clerics or any affectations which denote 'tokens of unstableness of mind'. Real spirituality should make people so normal and pleasant that 'each good man that saw them should be fain and joyful to have them in company'.

At a time when Aristotelian influence was at its height, in the Roman, not the Orthodox, branch of the Catholic Church, in the Scholasticism of the Middle Ages, Eckhart established a mystic-metaphysical school of thought similar to the direct-knowledge doctrine of the East and employed the negative characteristic of this doctrine: 'Fused yet not confused, founded yet not confounded'. Eckhart demonstrates the universal quality of mysticism. A. K. Coomaraswamy says that whole passages of Eckhart read like direct translations from Sanskrit; he is, in fact, universal and can be parallelled in the mysticism of all religions and all ages. His philosophy has been likened to that of Sankara, and it is pure Taoism when he says: 'It is permissible to take life's blessings with both hands, provided thou dost know thyself prepared in the opposite event to leave them just as gladly'. And again: 'Do not imagine you can ground your salvation upon actions; it must rest on what you *are*'. 'Indeed, I tell you the truth, any object you have in your mind, however good, will be a barrier between you and the inmost Truth.'

Eckhart has many affinities with Taoism, for one thing he was no other-worldly dreamer (a popular misconception of the nature of the mystic) but a man of administrative and literary capabilities, just as the Taoist Sage was often a man of great scholarship, a poet of genius, or even a government official. Also both are concerned with an intellectual rather than an emotional form of mysticism and with metaphysics rather than ethics. In Eckhart there is none of the feverish emotionalism and sensual states of rapture, of striving after

bliss or a personal relationship with the Beloved. His is the
cool, clearsighted way, rejecting fastings, vigils, asceticism and
the ecstatic visions so prevalent in his time.

> Satisfaction through feeling might mean that God sends us
> comfort, ecstasies and delights, but ... these are only a
> matter of emotion, but reasonable satisfaction is a purely
> spiritual process in which the highest summit of the soul
> remains unmoved by ecstasy, is not drowned in delight, but
> rather towers majestically above these. Man only finds
> himself in a state of spiritual satisfaction when these
> emotional storms of a psychical nature can no longer shake
> the summit of the soul.

'Those who are out for "feelings" or "great experiences", only
wish to have this pleasant side: that is self-will and nothing
else.'

Like Taoism, Eckhart lays stress on both the transcendence
and immanence of the Absolute, which Eckhart calls the
Godhead, as distinct from the triune God of Christianity, and
which can be equated with the Tao since Eckhart's Being
(wesen) is without differentiation or personality; it is the
Unknown, the utterly beyond, and is referred to in negative
terms as the Silence.

For Bruno, the Supreme, or the Divine, is an all-embracing
potentiality, incorporating the entire universe and all Being,
which cannot be comprehended by the finite mind or
intellect. Both Bruno and Nicholas of Cusa see the universe as
the limitless and perfect, permeated with the essence of beauty
and the opposites held in balance and harmony. 'In the two
extremes of the scale of nature we contemplate two principles
which are one ... two contraries which are harmonious and
the same. Therefore height is depth, the abyss is light
unvisited, darkness is brilliant, the large is small ....'[3] For
Bruno Nature is God revealed. Compare him with Chuang
Tzu on the subject – 'When subjective and objective are both
without their correlates, that is the very axis of Tao. And when
that axis passes through the centre at which all Infinities
converge, positive and negative alike blend into an infinite
One. Hence it has been said that there is nothing like the light
of nature'. And from the *Tao Te Ching* it is said of the One:

'Revealed, it is not dazzling; Hidden, it is not dark. Infinite, it cannot be defined. It goes back to non-existence ... meet it, you cannot see its face. Follow it, you cannot see its back'.[4]

Neo-Platonism penetrated Christianity through the Alexandrian centre of learning, and particularly through the work of Dionysius the Areopagite, and introduced negativism as a reaction to the over-positivism of the Aristotelian Scholastics, a negativism which, like that of the East, worked through a process of 'emptying, stripping bare and silencing the normal powers of the soul', which should result in a filling of the Spirit. Dionysius, who maintained that God transcends all contraries, wrote: 'At the last stage even the distinction between subject and object disappears and the Mind itself is That which it contemplates. Thought itself is transcended, and the whole object-realm vanishes. One subject now knows itself as the part and knows itself as the whole'.[5]

The Neo-Platonist conception of the universe begins with the One, the Good, which, like the Tao, is the source of all things; from it emanates the Intellect or Mind and from Mind proceeds the Soul, that is Man possessed, by reason of his origin, with a soul which, being a prisoner in the body, is dissatisfied with its limitations and begins the process of reversal of emanation in its return to the source from which it came. This is achieved through knowledge and in perfecting itself. Such a view-point is more other-worldly and serious than Taoism; the soul is a stranger in this world and the body a burden, as contrasted with the gamin-appreciation of life as expressed by Chuang Tzu and the Taoist poets, but the Neo-Platonist does not necessarily reject this world; it is God's world and therefore good and beautiful and to be valued rightly.

Plotinus, the great Neo-Platonist, spoke disparagingly of the body when he refused to have his portrait painted, saying: 'Is it not enough to have to bear the image in which nature has wrapped me without consenting to perpetuate the image of an image, as if it were worth contemplating?' He was no ascetic but, as Dean Inge wrote, 'fundamentally sane ... there were none of those attempts to force the pace which in many mystics produce those terrible reactions which are described as the dark night of the soul. This sense of dereliction, which fills so large a place in the mystics of the cloister, may have some connection with a deeper sense of guilt and sinfulness than the Neo-Platonist ever felt, but it is partly the effect of nervous over-strain and severe mortification of the body which Platonism never encouraged. Plotinus lived the active and sociable life of a professor amongst his pupils, but neither he nor his disciples tortured themselves like Suso and many other Catholic saints.' Plotinus was the supreme philosopher of Western mysticism, both theoretical and practical, maintaining that it is only when we use the highest faculties of our nature that we can become real or be in contact with Reality; this he calls 'the flight of the Alone to the Alone'. In his last words he said: 'I am striving to give back the Divine in myself to the Divine in the All'.

Among European mystics the English were reasonably free from the aberrations of psychic manifestations and erotic expression. Coventry Patmore, who calls the psychic phenomena of mysticism 'the frontiers between sense and spirit which are the devil's hunting ground', says:

> The true mystic does not set himself apart as someone specially endowed or favoured, he rigorously avoids what the author of *The Cloud of Unknowing* calls 'the monkey tricks of the soul'. He should be possessed with a lively sense of humour and sound good sense... there is nothing outwardly to distinguish a saint from an ordinary person ... the saint has no fads and you may live in the same house with him and never find that he is not a sinner like yourself, unless you ... obtrude lax ideas upon him and so provoke him to silence. He may impress you indeed by his harmlessness and imperturbable good humour and by never seeming to have much use for his time when it can be of service to you; but on the whole he will give you an agreeable impression of general inferiority to yourself. You must not, however, presume upon this inferiority so far as to offer him any affront, for he will be sure to answer you with some quiet and unexpected remark, showing a presence of mind arising, I suppose, from the presence of God, which will make you feel you have struck rock and only shaken your own shoulder.

The union of thought and emotion is best expressed in poetry in general and in metaphysical poetry in particular.

The English mystic poets, Donne, Crashaw, Traherne, Vaughan and Herbert share with Chuang Tzu and the Taoist poets a direct simplicity coupled with profound meaning, and in Wordsworth reached the height of understanding of, and communication with, Nature; for him it was an inseparable part of life, a unity and identification. 'I was often unable to think of external things as having an external existence, and I communed with all that I saw as something not apart from, but inherent in, my own immaterial nature.'[6] There were imparted to him

> Authentic tidings of invisible things;
> Of ebb and flow, and ever-enduring power;
> And central peace, subsisting at the heart
> Of endless agitation.[7]

Although Emily Brontë wrote one of the finest expressions of the mystic experience, her own realization seems to have fallen short in that it left none of the abiding joy characteristic of true mysticism. She felt the 'unuttered harmony' but also experienced a tumult of passion alien to it. Possibly this was due to what Swinburne spoke of as the 'dark unconscious instinct as of primitive nature worship' in her 'passionate great genius'. There is no greater testimony than the verses:

> With wide-embracing love
> Thy spirit animates eternal years,
> Pervades and broods above,
> Changes, sustains, dissolves, creates and rears.
>
> Though Earth and moon were gone
> And suns and universes ceased to be,
> And Thou wert left alone
> Every existence would exist in Thee.[8]

Yet the return to ordinary consciousness is painful for her: 'Oh dreadful is the check – intense the agony' for 'the soul to feel the flesh, and the flesh to feel the chain'. The same deficiency appears in Spenser, who finds that 'all that pleased earst now seems to paine' and that the return is one 'which loathing brings, of this vile world and these gay-seeming things'. The true joy and serenity of the mystic is lost. Contrast this with Traherne's abiding joy and delight in the world around: 'The corn was orient and immortal wheat, which never should be reaped nor ever sown. I thought it had stood from everlasting to everlasting. The dust and stones of the street were precious as gold; the gates were at first the end of the world. The green trees when I saw them first through one of the gates transported and ravished me, their sweetness and unusual beauty made my heart leap, and almost mad with ecstasy, they were such strange and wonderful things ... Eternity was manifest in the Light of Day, and something infinite behind everything appeared.'

But nearest of all to, and in fact indistinguishable from, the Taoist sage, is St Francis of Assisi, best described by Pier Pettignano who 'saw a vision of a superb procession of Apostles, Saints and Martyrs, with the Blessed Virgin at their head, all walking carefully and scrutinizing the ground with much earnestness, that they might tread as nearly as possible in the very footsteps of Christ. At the end of this pageant of the Church Triumphant came the little shabby figure of St Francis, bare-foot and brown-robed, and he alone was walking easily and strongly in the footsteps of our Lord.'

In Qabalism, the esoteric and mystic aspect of the Hebrew tradition, the Ain Soph is, like the Tao, expressed negatively and is its equivalent in that it is the supreme unconditioned, beyond finite understanding. It is the One which is without attributes; both immanent and transcendent, the ultimate mystery and, as in Taoism, 'that from which words turn back'. It has neither beginning nor end; it is the 'One without a second', the unlimited which includes all.

An analogy is maintained in the Sephiroth which emerge from the Ain Soph as the Ten Thousand Things arise from the Tao, containing all possibilities in the manifest world. The *yin-yang* balance is expressed in the Sephirotic Tree which has its positive right and negative left sides, the light and active and the dark and passive aspects, and duality runs through it, each sephiroth being the complement of its opposite and each containing within itself the germ of its contrary but complementary aspect. Like the *yin* and the *yang* the sephirotic pairs retain their distinctive qualities while being inseparable.

This makes the doctrine of balance, harmony and equilibrium basic to Qabalism which maintains the *yin-yang* symbolism throughout. 'The balance denoteth the male and female' and 'whilst the equilibrium existeth there is intercommunication between them and they are joined together in One'.[9] 'All things which are in the Microproscopus have part good and part evil, right and left, Mercy and Judgement.'[10] Man is born in two halves, so that throughout life male and female each search for the complementary 'other half'. The *yang* and the *yin* are also represented in duality as the King and Queen, while the two-headed King-Queen symbolizes the androgynous being, having attained unity. This bridges the gap between the Absolute, the Ain Soph the Unknowable, and the finite universe, the sphere of the Ten Thousand Things.

The realm of duality is a reflected world which makes the invisible temporarily visible, which is one of the meanings of the oft-quoted 'as above, so below'. This doctrine of *maya* is expressed in the 'vanities' of Solomon which mirror, or reflect, the divine Reality, but being reflections, or aspects, they are of the nature of illusions, inseparable from creation.

The 'dark void' of Qabalism has affinities with the Tao as 'the Mother of all things' since it is from thence that all things emanate and from it that the light emerges.

Other points of similarity between Qabalism and Taoism are that man is regarded as the intermediary, in Qabalism reconciling and reintegrating God and his creation and in Taoism between the powers of Heaven and Earth; he is the central point between the worlds or states as in the sephirotic symbolism the left side and right side have the middle pillar as the resolving third, just as in the active and passive aspects of the Triple Head, Kether, the Supreme Crown, is the resolving third. The existential opposites are reconciled in the Divine.

Qabalism also recognizes levels of awareness. *Yesod* is that of the ordinary limited individual and must be transcended and the state of *Tiphereth* reached to become aware of and to watch the actions and reactions of the lower state. Attaining to this level brings equilibrium and harmony and an indifference to worldly things and to praise or blame.

As in Taoism everything emerges from the Tao and returns to it, so in Qabalism all comes from God and returns to God; it returns, in fact, to a point or ground it has never in reality left.

The exoteric aspect of the monotheistic religions lacks the balance of the male-female divinities which appear in all ancient religions of the world in which each deity has his or her counterpart. Exoteric Judaism, Christianity and Islam suffer from an over-balance of an essentially masculine God; he is God the Father to the exclusion of the consort Mother Goddess. This masculine God is also separate from his creation. But the early Christian sect of the Gnostics, which probably had pre-Christian associations, some authorities seeing in it still earlier Zoroastrian, Babylonian and Jewish influences, wrote in its scriptures of the Divinity–'From Thee, Father and through Thee Mother'. Valentinus, a member of this sect which was later regarded by the Church as a heresy, said that although God is beyond expression yet the divine may be considered as being both male and female, with the Father as Depth and the Ineffable and the Mother as Grace and Silence, each complementing the other, though, again, in the words of the *Tao Te Ching*, the female principle is 'the Mother of All'. *The Apocraphon of John* says: 'She existed before them all, the mother-father', and in *The Trimorphic Protenoia* a divine voice says 'I am androgynous'.

Modern discovery of ancient Gnostic texts reveals a closer connection between early Christian sects and eastern religions than is evident in the accounts left by orthodox Christianity. There seems to have been an Eastern influence of a distinctly Hindu-Buddhist attitude to sin, which may have entered Gnosticism through the gymnasophists, as the Greeks called them. In the Gnostic Gospels there is no preoccupation with sin and guilt; instead there is the Eastern attitude that sin can be equated with ignorance. This ignorance can be remedied by gnosis, the search for self-knowledge and awareness. When anyone 'comes to have knowledge his ignorance vanishes by itself, as the darkness vanishes when light appears, so also the deficiency vanishes in the fulfilment'.[11] The Gnostics recognized the limitations of the finite mind and their aim was enlightenment, attained through direct, individual relationship with the deity; a living, existential experience of 'the Living One'. This was the only valid 'knowledge' and it required harmony, spontaneity, openness and awareness which led to final unity. To 'enter the Kingdom ... you make the two one, and the inside like the outside and the outside like the inside, and the above like the below and ... the male and the female one and the same'.[12]

The male and the female, like the Two Great Powers, are complementary and the two together are responsible for the emanations of pairs of harmonious energies: 'Mother, father, unity, being a source of the entire circle of existence'.[13]

There is an element of world-renunciation in Gnosticism which is paralleled in Buddhism but alien to classical Taoism – the body is referred to as 'poverty' and the spirit as 'wealth' in the *Gospel of Thomas*. On the other hand, Gnosticism sees harmony in creation and joins with all Eastern religions and philosophies in seeing the divine and its creation as One. It also brings the universal message 'awake thou that sleepest' – 'end the sleep which weighs heavy upon you, depart from the oblivion which fills you with darkness'.[14] This is the start of the journey which leads to gnosis and enlightenment.

As Taoism protested against the extreme conventionalism of Confucianism, so it was said that the Sufi movement was a revolt against the luxury, loose-living and mechanical religion of the Caliphs and their entourages; but Sufism was also held to have originated in the experiences of the Prophet himself and to exist in the Qur'an, which contains elements of potential mysticism and exercises orientated towards union with the Divine – the whole essence of mysticism. In either case, the fact remains that the Sufis have been responsible for some of the finest mystical poetry in the world. Monasticism, which produced much of the mystical literature of Buddhism and Christianity, being forbidden by the Prophet, a system of saints, sages and an iniatic master-pupil relationship was instituted. The Way, for the novice, is based, as in Taoism, Hinduism and Buddhism, on the Sage, Guru, Master or Sheik dependency, since the Way can be dangerous without expert guidance. In Islam, probably more than in other religious branches of mysticism, the quest for union takes the form of a journey towards God; the Sufi speaks of different states as 'stations' which are arrived at only by unremitting effort, or, in al-Ghazali's words, 'spiritual application' on the part of the follower of the Way, as contrasted with advancement which comes not so much through personal effort as by Divine Grace. 'Thou must persevere until He mingles Himself with thy Soul, and thine own individual existence passes out of sight.'[15] In all mysticism the personality is transcended and disappears, all distinctions cease to exist: 'duality ceases and unity appears. He remains and you do not, or He passes away in you and you remain and He does not. Or else both of you pass away in God and pay no attention to yourselves, and that is perfection.' 'I and Thou signify duality, and duality is an illusion, for Unity alone is Truth'.[16] Or, as al-Hallaj said: 'I am Thyself'.

The way of the Sufi is that of gnosis. While the Will is the salient factor in Christianity, it is the Intellect which takes the premier place in Islam. The mystic knowledge of God is obtained through Knowledge. All trace of self must be lost in the Divine Essence. As al-Hallaj said: 'To say "I" and "God" is to deny the unity of God ... lover, beloved and love are one'. He maintained that he did not feel the dual nature of man.

Ibn Arabi expresses the mystic oneness of all life in: 'My heart has opened to every form; it is a pasture for gazelles, a cloister for Christian monks, a temple for idols, the Ka'ba of the pilgrims, the Tables of the Torah and the book of the Qoran. I practise the religion of Love in whatsoever directions its caravans advance, the religion of Love shall be my religion and my faith'.

Islamic mysticism tends to renounce the world and its attachments and the element of asceticism is present, but it is a matter of choice as to whether it is put into practice or not.

In Islam there are the ninety-nine Names of God, but the hundredth, the last, is the un-namable, the undifferentiated, Pure Being, the One, and like the Tao it is also that from which all emerges, the container of all possibilities. Al-Ghazali, who like Taoists and Buddhists, believed that God could not be found by speculation and study, says that Primordial Truth cannot be searched for since it is present and visible; the result of searching for it is to make it invisible and hidden. This parallels Chuang Tzu's 'Those who would find Tao through study look for that which cannot be studied; those who would obtain the Tao through effort try for that which cannot be obtained by effort; those who would reach the Tao by reason look for that which cannot be found in reason'.

But mystics of all ages and creeds speak with one voice finally, whether it be the Western metaphor of the drop returning to the ocean, or the Eastern expression of the ocean being poured into the drop, all are equally explicit in 'Foregoing self, the Universe grows I', and the Hermetic: 'That which is below is like that which is above, and that which is above is like that which is below for the performance of the miracles of the One Substance.' This is the basic teaching of all mysticism, that the Microcosm and Macrocosm are but reflections of each other and are One.

NOTES

1   1   H.G. Creel, *What is Taoism?*, Chicago (1970).
     2   *The Ancient Sage*
     3   Takakusu, Junjiro. *The Essentials of Buddhist Philosophy* (1967).
     4   *Bhagavad Gita*, III.34.
     5   Takakusu. XLVIII. 376.
     6   *Bhagavad Gita*. 13.30.
     7   Li Chi. XXI. 2.1. *Record of Rites.* Confucian texts from the last century B.C.
     8   *The Doctrine of the Mean.* Trans. Legge.
     9   Jinsai, *Dojï-mon.*

2   1   *Tao Te Ching*, 40.
     2   *Tao Te Ching*, 25.
     3   *Fourfold Root of the Principle of Sufficient Reason*, Leideng (1889).
     4   Chuang Tzu, Ch. 23. Trans. Legge.
     5   J. Needham, *Time and Knowledge in China and the West.*
     6   *The Book of Lieh Tzu.*
     7   Tung Chung-shu. Confucian scholar of Han Dynasty, responsible for establishing Confucianism as the state religion.

3   1   Analects, XII, 2.
     2   Analects, IV, 28.
     3   *Tales of Rabbi Nachman.* Souvenir Press (1974).
     4   H.G. Creel, *What is Taoism?*, Chicago Univ. Press (1970).
     5   *The Life of Oscar Wilde.* London (1946).
     6   *Sadhana.* Mahayanist Buddhist scripture.
     7   *Stones of Venice.*
     8   *Magna Moralia.* 1211a.
     9   E. Conze, *Further Buddhist Studies.*
    10   Bhagavad Gita.

4   1   *Baudhayana-Dharmasutra*, 3.1.24.
     2   Emerson, *The Over-Soul.*
     3   *The Bugbear of Democracy, Freedom and Equality. Studies in Comparative Religion*, Summer 1977.

5   1   Michael Sullivan, *The Birth of Landscape Painting in China.* R.K.P. 1962.
     2   From the *Hua shan-shui hsu.* Preface to painting by Tsung Ping.
     3   From the *Yüan Yeh*, a Ming treatise on gardening.
     4   Yang Yap & A. Cotterell, *The Early Civilization of China.*

5   *Principles of Chinese Painting,* Princeton, 1947.
6   Pairs of tablets were inscribed with parallel quotations which corresponded in tonal value and content.
7   The *Yüan Yeh.*
8   The *Yüan Yeh.*
9   The *Yüan Yeh.*
10 The *Yüan Yeh.*
11 The *Yüan Yeh.*
12 *Gardens of China.*
13 The treatise *P'ing Shih* by Yüan Chung-lang.
14 *Man and Nature,* Allen & Unwin, 1968.

6   1   H. Wilhelm. *Change, Eight Lectures on the I Ching.* R.K.P. 1975.
    2   Indian Philosophy.
    3   Tao Te Ching. XVI. Trans. Chung-yuan Chang.
    4   *Gifts of Unknown Things.* Hodder & Stoughton, 1976.

7   1   Thich Nhat Hanh. *Zen Keys.*
    2   The Ch'an Master Ts'ao Shan
    3   Hui-neng, the Sixth Patriarch.
    4   The Altar-Sutra.
    5   E.R. Dodds. *The Greeks and the Irrational.* Univ. of California. 1951.
    6   *Life Beyond Death.*
    7   Emerson. Circles.
    8   J. Needham. *Science and Civilization in China.* Vol. II.
    9   *Small is Beautiful.*

8   1   Brihadaranyaka. 4. 4-10.
    2   Isa Upanishad, 9.11.
    3   *Studies of the English Mystics.*
    4   *Bhagavad Gita.* VI. 30.
    5   W.R. Inge. op. cit.

11 1   Vivekananda. *Collected Works.*
    2   *Shvetashvatara Upanishad.*
    3   *Chhandogya Upanishad.*
    4   Sen T'sen. Third Patriarch of the Ch'an School of Buddhism.
    5   *Bhagavad Gita.* IX.
    6   *Katha Upanishad.*
    7   Ch. 18.

[8]   III.4.
[9]   *Bhagavad Gita.* III.19.

12 [1]   Visuddhimagga, XV. 43.
    [2]   *The Sermon at Benares.*
    [3]   *Majjhima-Nikaya.*
    [4]   *Udana.* 80.
    [5]   *Nagarjuna Madhymika Karika.* XXV.
    [6]   Altar Sutra of the 6th Patriarch.
    [7]   *Altar Sutra.*
    [8]   *Altar Sutra.*
    [9]   *Shen-pu-mieh-lun.* On the Indestructibility of the Soul.
    [10] Tao Te Ching. XXV.
    [11] *An Introduction to Tantric Buddhism.*

13 [1]   *The Teachings of the Magi.*
    [2]   Shikand-Gumani Vazar. III.
    [3]   Hseih-ho, on the Canons of Art
    [4]   Tao Te Ching, Ch. 1.
    [5]   Ch. VIII.
    [6]   *The Gathas.*

14 [1]   *Centuries of Meditation.*
    [2]   Christian Ethics.
    [3]   *De rerum natura.*
    [4]   Ch. XIV.
    [5]   *The Celestial Hierarchy.*
    [6]   In a note on *Ode to Intimations of Immortality.*
    [7]   *The Excursion.* Bk. IV.
    [8]   *No Coward Soul is Mine.*
    [9]   *The Book of Concealed Mystery.* 33.
    [10] *Qabalah* Ch. XXXIII.
    [11] *The Gospel of Truth.*
    [12] *The Gospel of Thomas.*
    [13] *Hippolytus.* 6.17.
    [14] *Teachings of Solomon.*
    [15] Jami, Nur al-Din. Fifteenth-century Sufi Afghan poet and philosopher.
    [16] Abn Yazid al-Bistami. Ninth-century Sufi philosopher.

INDEX